Holiday Crafts

196 Crafts for Mother's Day, Father's Day, Valentine's Day, 4th of July, Halloween Crafts, Thanksgiving Crafts, & Christmas Crafts!

by Kitty Moore

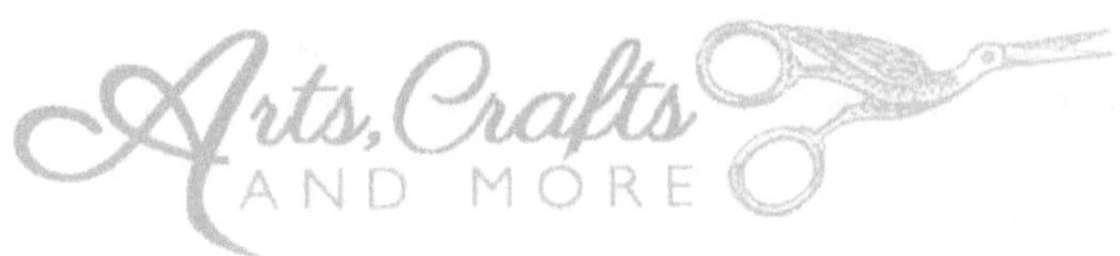

Table of Contents

Introduction

Holidays would never be complete without all the fabulous decorations and holiday crafts – they are what really makes each holiday festive and special in its own way.

Whether you are looking forward to a big Thanksgiving dinner or celebrating the 4th of July, there can be no doubt that part of the fun is in making the holiday for ourselves and our loved ones.

Now, I know that we are all busy people and that, as a result, we may just fall back on commercial decorations but this is largely as a result of a lack of knowledge about home-crafts.

Be honest, when I said home-made, you were picturing the pair of toilet tube binoculars that your toddler made at pre-school, weren't you? Either that or visions of dining tables covered with paper and glitter getting everywhere.

The really great news is that there is no need to stress when it comes to making your own holiday crafts - I have compiled this compendium of crafts for all of the major holidays.

To make it into this compilation, crafts have to be reasonably quick or reasonably simple to do – you will not need to take a course in stained glass techniques to do the crafts in this book. At the same time, however, I also realize that there are going to be people who are more advanced in terms of craft skills and so all the projects in this book can, with a little imagination be taken up a notch.

Even the most advanced crafters are going to be able to pick up some useful hints and great projects from this book. You will be taught how to create home-made decorations that make the store-bought ones look cheap and nasty.

Sit back, relax and be inspired by this mammoth collection of crafts – there is a bit of everything in here so go craft crazy!

Craft 1: Red, White and Blue Decorations for The 4th of July: Garden Glory

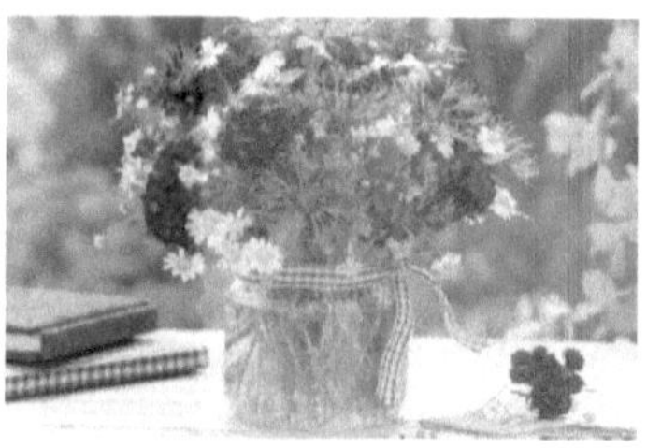

Materials

- Vases
- Ribbon
- Flowers

Directions

1. Get some wildflowers from your garden or other simple blooms having patriotic colors (red, white and blue) from a flower shop. Neatly arrange them in a nice vase as shown above. To finish, tie a snappy gingham ribbon around the vase.

Craft 2: Colorful Star Stickers

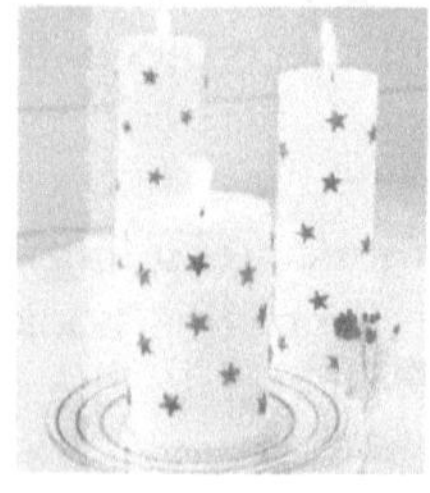

Materials

- Candles
- Star-shaped (colored stickers)

Directions

1. Get some red, white and blue stickers and stick them to candles as desired. These are best displayed on a white tablecloth with stars on it.

Craft 3: American Flag Burlap Banner

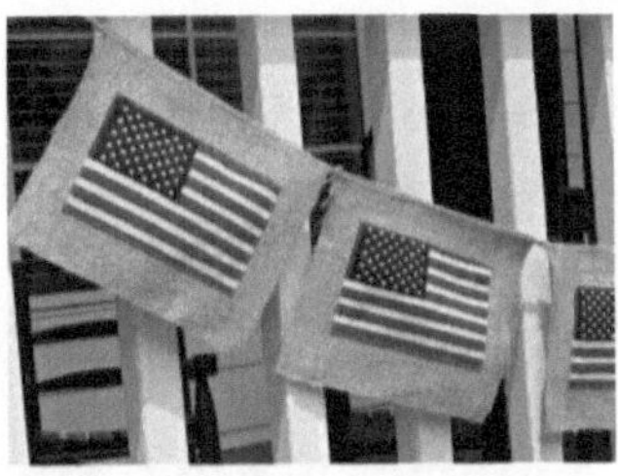

Materials

- Burlap sacks
- Small American flags
- A rope

Directions

1. Cut a burlap sack into a number of squares and stitch small, square-shaped American flags on them. Join them together by passing a thin rope through the folded edge of each burlap square. You can hang the long rope anywhere conspicuous in your house: living room or dinner room, the choice is yours!

Craft 4: Red, White and Blue Crepe Paper and Lights

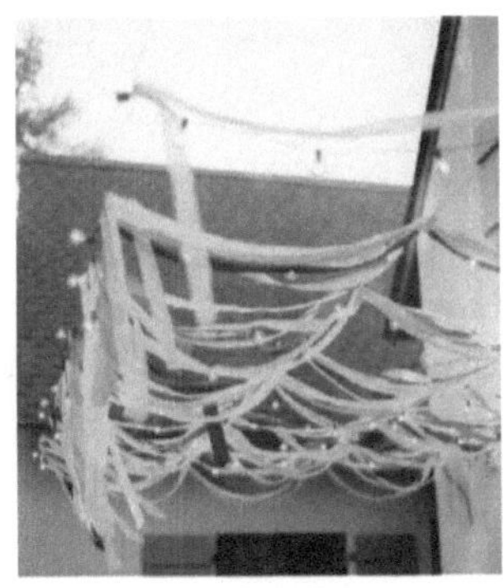

Materials

- Crepe papers in red, white and blue
- Lights

Directions

1. Cut the Crepe papers into long, rectangular strips. Arrange them to form the red, white and blue stripes alternately. Attach some Christmas light-like bulbs to different parts of the colored Crepe papers. When they are lighted, it becomes a beautiful spectacle.

Craft 5: American Flag Mason Jars

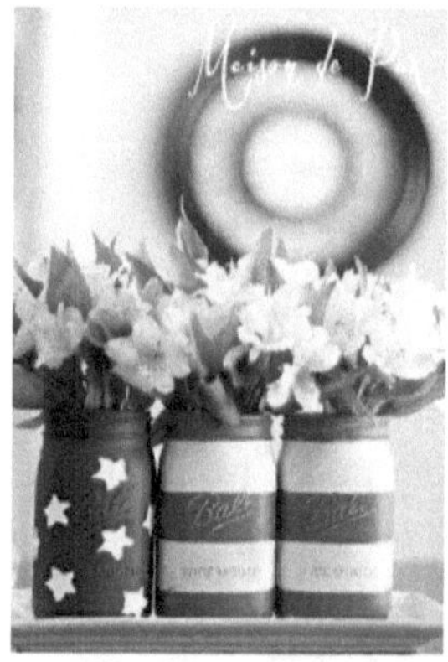

Materials

- Mason jars painted in American flag colors
- Some flowers

Directions

1. Use the mason jars painted in American flag colors as your flower vase and choose some pretty flowers to arrange in them. If you cannot find the readymade jars, all you need to do is to paint your own using acrylic paint in red white and blue, using the above picture as a reference.

I have included a bonus just for you…

FOR A LIMITED TIME ONLY – Get my best-selling book "DIY Crafts: The 100 Most Popular Crafts & Projects That Make Your Life Easier" absolutely FREE!

Readers who have downloaded the bonus book as well have seen the greatest changes in their crafting abilities and have expanded their repertoire of crafts – so it is *highly recommended* to get this bonus book today!

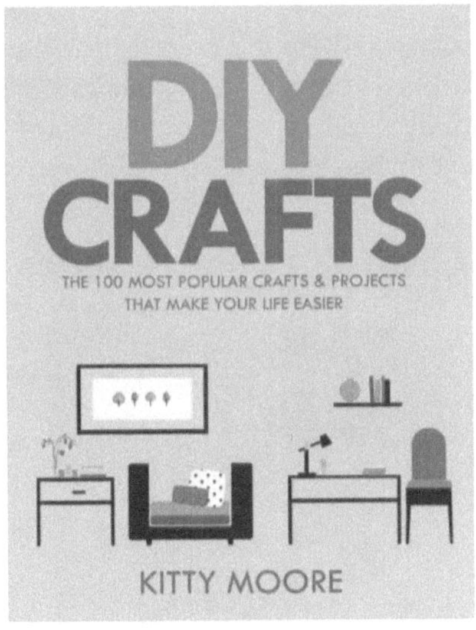

Get your free copy at:

ArtsCraftsAndMore.com/Bonus

Craft 6: Paper Stars

Materials

- Red, white and blue papers
- Scissors

Directions

1. Grab your scissors and cut the colored papers into stars of different shapes. If you like, you can vary their designs. You can use these paper stars to decorate your bulletin board or arrange them on wallpapers in your bedroom or your children's bedrooms.

Craft 7: Paper Rosettes

Materials

- Paper in red, white and blue
- Scissors
- A tape rule
- Brads or adhesive stars

- A blank wreath
- Blank card or felt circles

Directions

1. Cut your paper into equal-sized squares – the bigger the square, the bigger the rosette will be. You will need 2-3 squares per rosette. Accordion fold the squares until you have strips that measure around 1-inch wide.

2. Fold each strip in half. Glue one half to the next so that you form a fan shape. Open out and see whether or not your rosette is full enough. If not, glue on a third strip.

3. When you are happy that the rosette is full enough, glue the remaining two sides together and adhere to the paper or felt circle. Cover the center hole of the rosette with a brad or star. Glue onto the wreath base until it is covered.

Craft 8: 4th of July Bunting

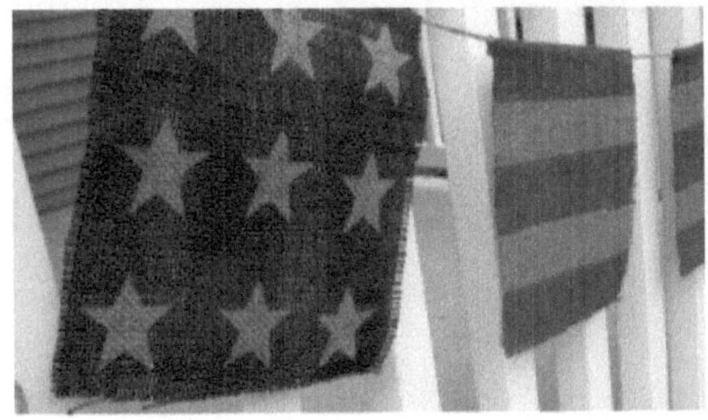

Materials

- Burlap
- Foam stars
- Masking tape
- Acrylic paint in red and blue
- Twine
- A hot glue gun
- Double sided tape

Directions

1. Cut the burlap into evenly sized rectangles – one set of three rectangles will form a set, so cut in multiples of three. Taking the first rectangle, lay out your foam stars in even rows so that you get a similar look to the one in the picture, leaving about a ½ inch space at the top edge as your "seam" allowance. When satisfied, stick them in place with a little double-sided tape. (Just enough so that they don't move – we'll be pulling them off afterwards.)

2. Paint the blue background, using the stars as a kind of negative stencil and set aside to dry. Take the next piece of burlap and mask out evenly spaced stripes similar to what we have in the picture above, leaving about a ½ inch space at the top edge as your "seam" allowance. Using red paint, paint in your stripes and set aside to dry. Repeat on the third piece of burlap. Do as many sets as you want to and when they are dry, lay them right side down in the following order – Blue, red, red.

3. Lay down a line of glue at the top edge and then lay your twine over it. Fold over and secure with more glue if necessary. Repeat with all the rectangles and your bunting is ready.

Craft 9: 4th of July Tinted Mason Jars

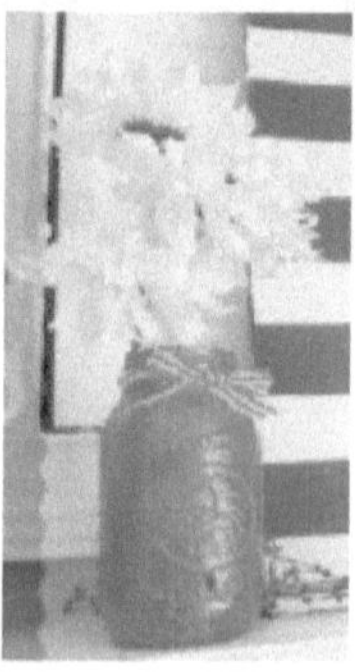

Materials

- 3 Mason jars
- Food coloring in red and blue
- Chalk paint in white
- Modge Podge

- Paper in red, white and blue
- Three ramekins

Directions

1. Make sure that the jars are clean and dry. Put a few tablespoons of water into each of the ramekins. Each color will have its own ramekin. Put about a tablespoon of food coloring into two of the ramekins and a tablespoon of chalk paint into the third. Place about two tablespoons of Modge Podge into each of the mason jars.

2. Add the contents of the ramekins into each separate jar and twirl so that the color and Modge Podge mix well. Swirl the mixture higher and higher along the sides until the inside is completely coated. Pour any residue back into the relevant ramekin. Turn the jars upside down and let the excess drain on absorbent towel.

3. Place a sheet of wax paper on a flat baking tray and preheat your over to around 225 degrees. Set the jars out on this, again upside down. Leave for around 10 minutes before turning them right-side up. (Be careful, they will be hot.) Bake for another half an hour. If the finish looks streaky, put them back in the oven for another 15 minutes. If you are not happy with the color, repeat the process.

Craft 10: Floating USA Balloons

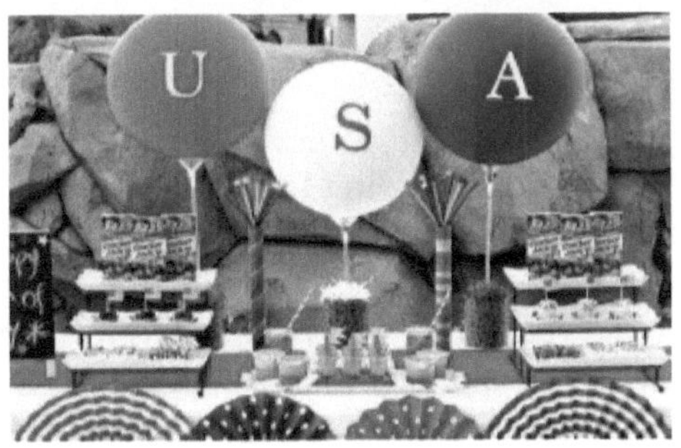

Materials

- Balloons
- Paints
- Drinking straws

Directions

1. Inflate your three balloons (their sizes depend on what you want).
    It is advisable to buy red, white and blue balloons and you will
    have to carefully paint "U S A" on them. Insert the edge of each
    balloon into a drinking straw and let the straw stand in a can
    stuffed with paper or plastic cuttings.

Craft 11: 4th of July Tablecloths

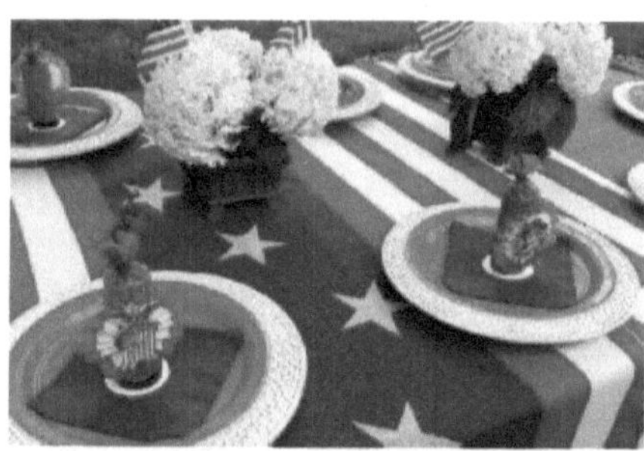

Materials

-   Good fabric for tablecloths, such as linen, cotton, silk, organza,
-   Polyester and vinyl in red, white and blue
-   Scissors
-   Paper, fabric or foam stars in white

Directions

1. Separate your fabric according to color. Start Cut the red and white
    fabric into strips and sew together to form the striped part of the
    flag, remembering that some of the strips will be longer than the
    others - use the flag as a reference. Lay out the blue fabric and cut
    to size. Sew this to the red and white fabric. Sew or glue on the
    stars to the blue rectangle.

Craft 12: Patriotic Felt Wreaths

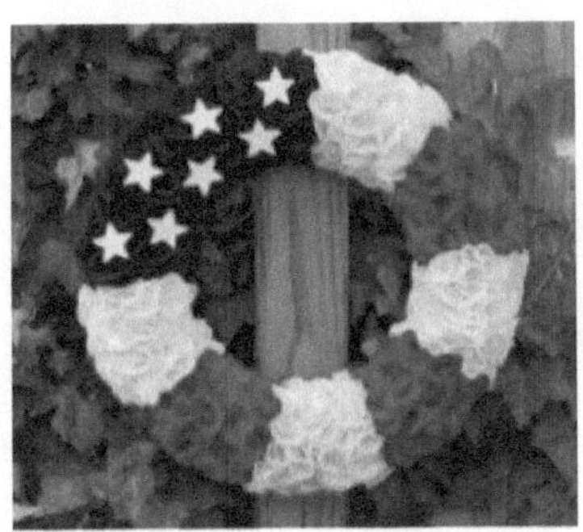

Materials

- Creased color fabric
- Thread and needle
- Cloth stars

Directions

1. You can buy at least **8** pieces of creased colored fabric or you can just buy the plain colored fabric and crease it yourself by folding it sideways and tacking it with a thread using a thin needle.

2. You can choose to sew the stars on the cloth or buy the fabric that already has stars on it. With your needle, join the pieces of creased clothing together until a circular shape is formed. Hang the patriotic felt wreath anywhere in your house.

Craft 13: 4th of July Make-up

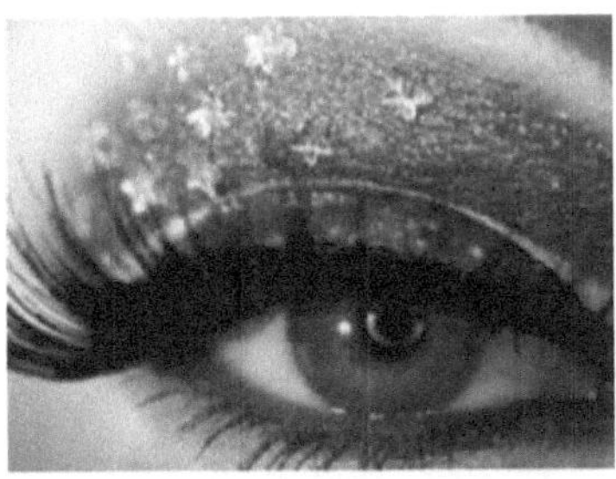

Materials

- Eye shadow palette with red, white and blue, preferably metallic

- Eye shadow brush
- Adhesive stars (For use on skin)
- Dark blue eyeliner
- Dark blue mascara

Directions

1. Get creative with your make-up on the 4th of July. One of the craziest things beautiful women do now on the 4th of July is to look amazing on this special day.

2. Grab your eye shadow palette. Apply the colors as shown in the picture above: in red, white and blue colors. If you have a shiny one in your eye shadow palette, do not hesitate to use it! For an even more intense effect, wet your eye shadow brush before dipping it into the eye shadow. Finish off with lashings of eye liner and mascara.

Craft 14: Paper Lanterns

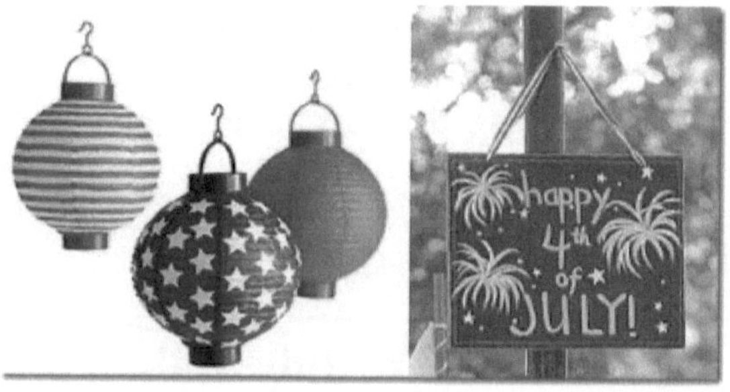

Materials

- Red, white and blue paper lanterns
- White adhesive stars

Directions

1. You can easily obtain paper lanterns from the shopping mall. What is very important is the way you arrange it. Each paper lantern has a hook with which you can hang it from the ceiling of your living room, bedroom or dining room. Adhere the stars to your blue

lantern and hang them up in groups of three – one red, one white and one blue.

Craft 15: Patriotic Upcycled Can Flower Pots

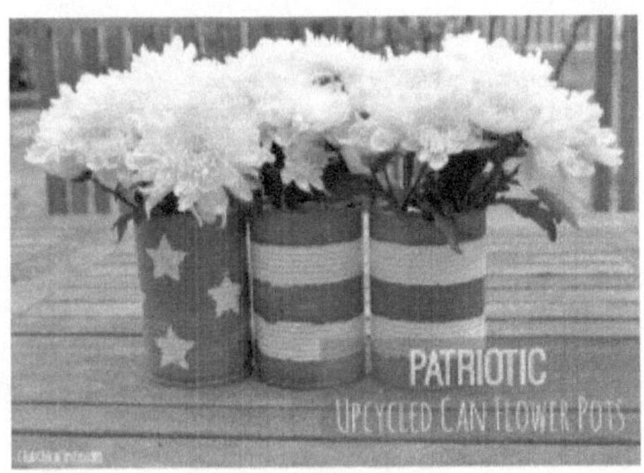

Materials

- Recycled cans
- Small plants
- Pebbles
- Potting soil
- Paints

Directions

1. Use some recycled tomato or fruit cans. Cut out the top edge making sure that there are no sharp edges. Paint one can blue and the other two cans white and set aside to dry. Once dry, paint stars onto the blue can and red stripes onto the other two cans. Set aside to dry. Punch some holes in the bottom of the cans to facilitate drainage.

2. Place a layer of pebbles in the bottom of the cans. Fill up to halfway with potting soil and then place your plant into the can. Fill the rest of the space is filled in with potting soil and pat down so that the plant is securely in place. Place on the driveway or your lawn and water – this prevents the inside of your house getting soiled by the excess water.

Craft 16: Hand-made Stars and Stripes Beach Ball

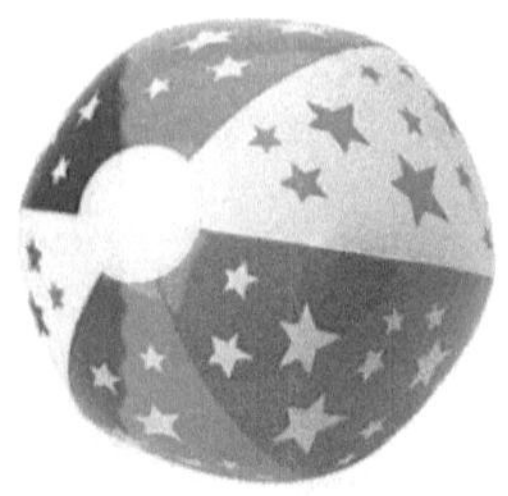

Materials

- Pieces of colored leather with stars and stripes on them
- Scissors
- Foam

Directions

1. Cut the leather into panels that can be sewed together to form a hand-made beach ball. Cut circular pieces to close over the top and bottom points. Arrange the panels as desired and then sew them together. Only sew one of the circles on at this stage. Fill the ball with foam until it has a nice, solid shape. Then sew the circular, topmost part.

Craft 17: Patriotic Manicure

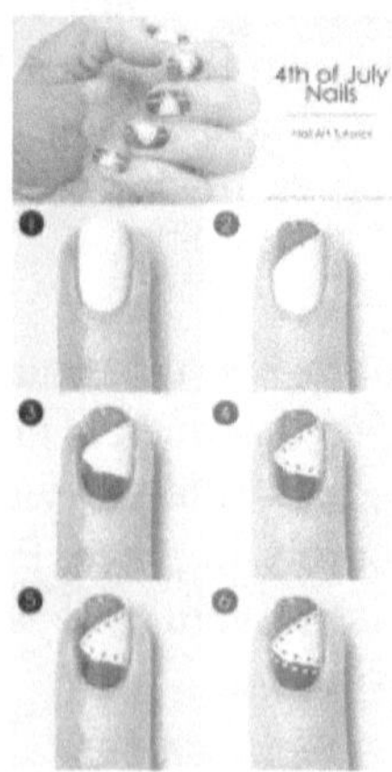

Materials

- Nail varnish in red, white and blue
- A nail art brush
- A toothpick
- Cello tape

Directions

1. Paint the whole nail white and allow it to dry completely. Place a piece of cello tape over the nail, starting at the midpoint and working at a 45-degree angle to the opposite edge of the nail. Only the top bit of your nail will be uncovered. Paint this section red and allow this to dry thoroughly.

2. Remove the tape and repeat the process, this time slanting the tape down towards the inner corner of the nail and paint with blue nail varnish. Allow to dry thoroughly. Using the toothpick, make a line of dots at the edge of each section as shown in the picture above. Once dry, finish with a clear topcoat.

Craft 18: 4th of July Face Painting

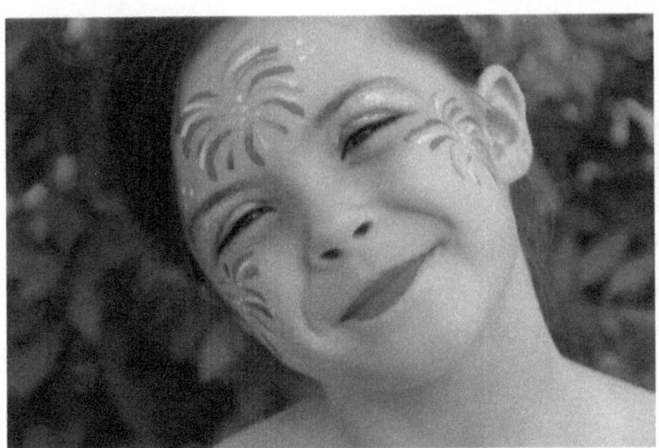

Materials

- Face paint in red, white and blue
- A makeup sponge (optional)
- Paint brush

Directions

1. Paint one half of your face blue and the other half white. Allow to dry. Paint white stars onto the blue side. Paint red stripes onto the white side. Alternatively, paint an American flag in full on each cheek or, instead of painting the design over the whole face, follow the steps above, just painting the cheeks.

Craft 19: 4th of July Statement Chair

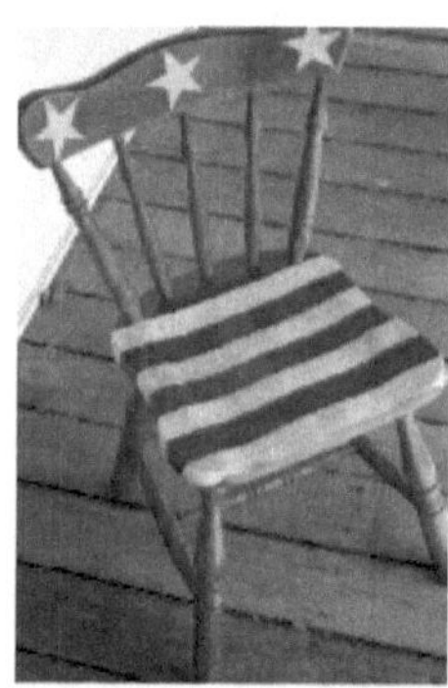

Materials

- An old wooden kitchen chair
- A star stencil
- Acrylic paint in red, white and blue
- Sandpaper
- Wood sealer
- Masking tape or duct tape
- Paint brush
- Stencil brush or sponge

Directions

1. Sand off old varnish as necessary and wipe off any residue dust. Paint the legs and seat of the chair red and set aside to dry. Mask off stripes on the seat of the chair, extending to the sides of the seat as well. Paint in your white stripes, taking care not to splash the legs of the chair. Allow to dry and apply another coat if necessary before removing masking tape.

2. Cover the seat of the chair with newspaper to protect it and paint the backrest of the chair blue. Set aside to dry. Mask your stencil in place on the top of the chair's backrest and paint on your stars in the same way as done above and set aside to dry. Finish off with two coats of sealer for a lasting finish.

Craft 20: Stained Glass Soaps

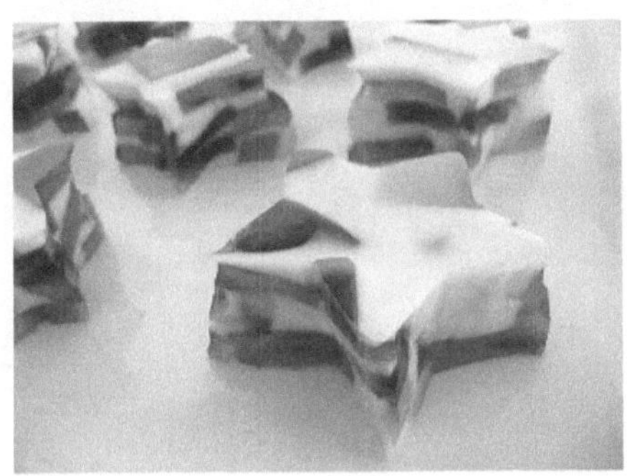

Materials

- Melt and pour soaps in red, white and blue
- A silicone ice-cube mold in the shape of a star
- A microwave
- A disposable microwave container that can handle high temperatures
- A knife
- Cellophane

Directions

1. Roughly chop the pieces of soap into chunks that are about the same size. Reserve about a third of the white soap and then layer the rest of the chunks in the molds, taking care to that all the colors are represented. Place the trays in the freezer. Then take a bit of the white soap and place it in the microwave container.

2. Microwave on high for about 20 seconds until it melts. Rather do short bursts of 20 seconds at a time or you risk burning the soap. When the white soap has melted, remove the molds from the freezer and top up the molds with the hot soap. This will help to

hold all your colors in place. Set aside to cool off and wrap with cellophane to prevent moisture beads forming on the soap.

Craft 21: Star Streamer Garland

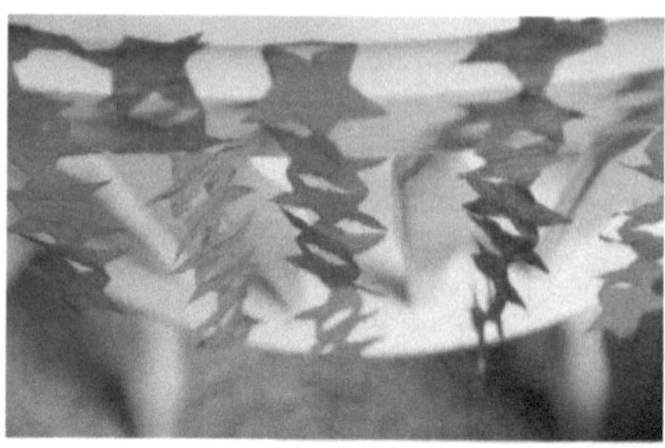

Materials

- Colored papers
- Scissors
- Glue

Directions

1. Cut out red, white and blue stars from the colored papers. Use glue to join them together. You can the tape them to your walls or to bulletin boards.

Craft 22: Faux Tie-Dye Pillow

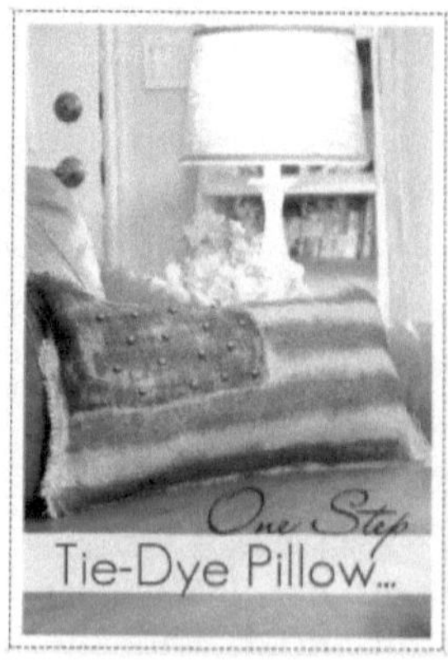

Materials

- White burlap
- A sewing machine
- Fabric paints
- A paint brush
- A rag or absorbent paper
- Brads

Directions

1. Your burlap should be about double the length that you want your cushion to be and also have an inch seam allowance on each side. The look here is shabby chic so you are not going to use a very loaded paint brush. Draw the flag on the front half of the cushion cover using a sharp pencil.

2. Now it is time to paint. Start by painting on the blue rectangle of the flag. Brush quickly and lightly so that some of the burlap shows through. Use plain or star-shaped brads to represent the stars of the flag. Sew up your cushion cover and you are all done.

Craft 23: Hanging Board

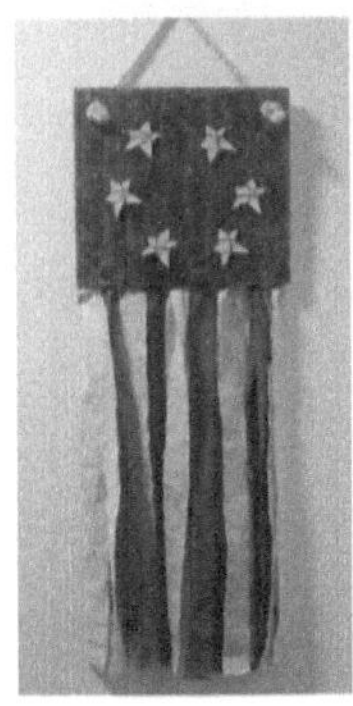

Materials

- Pieces of cloth in red and white
- A wooden board
- Blue acrylic paint
- Paper stars

- Tacks, nails or glue
- Rope
- A drill

Directions

1. Drill a hole into each of the top corners of the board – big enough for the rope to fit through. Paint the board blue and set aside to dry. If you like, distress it a little to give it more character. Tear the fabric into evenly sized strips and the nail or glue them to the bottom edge of the board. (The edge opposite where you drilled the holes.) Glue your paper stars onto the blue board. Thread the rope through the holes and knot on the front to secure.

Craft 24: Patriotic Tablescape

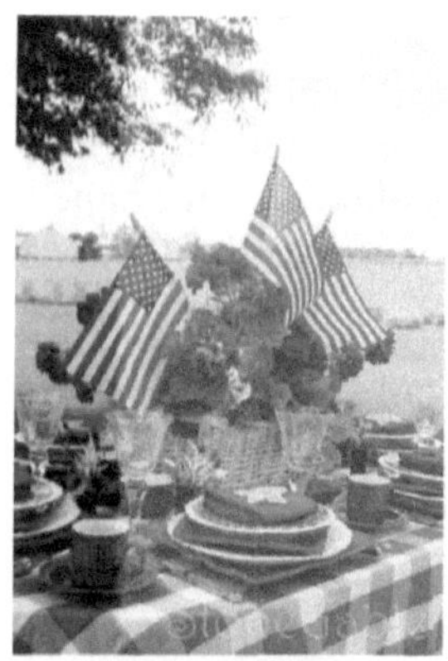

Materials

- American flags
- Patriotic tablecloth
- Arrangement of red and white flowers

Directions

1. Drape your dining table with a tablecloth in red, white and blue. Arrange the flowers around your flags. The arrangement should be the tallest on the table.

Craft 25: 4th of July Poster

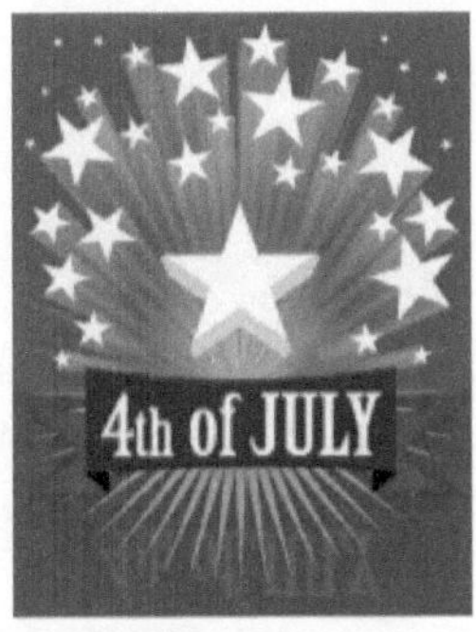

Materials

- Paper
- Colored paints
- Pencils
- Scissors

Directions

1. Either draw a basic template for your poster or download one online. Fill it in with bright colored, bold paint in red, white and blue. Leave some areas of the poster blank so that the white paper dazzles through – ideal for stars and stripes.

Craft 26: Patriotic Cups

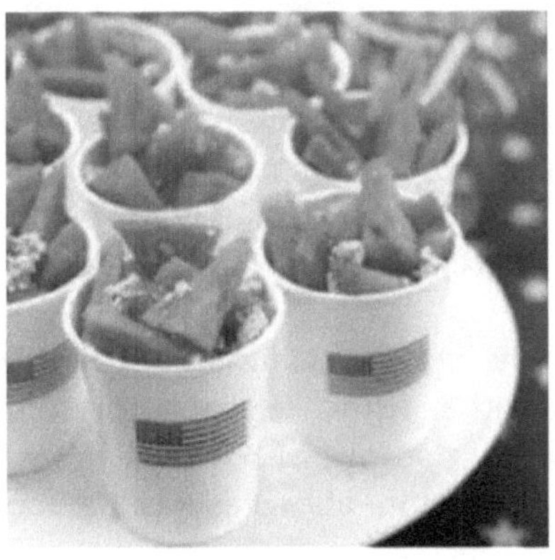

Materials

- Plastic white cups
- Adhesive flag stickers

Directions

1. Make sure that the cups are clean of any residue and completely dry. Adhere the flag stickers to the center of the front of the cups and they are ready to use.

Craft 27: Easy 4th Of July Nail Art

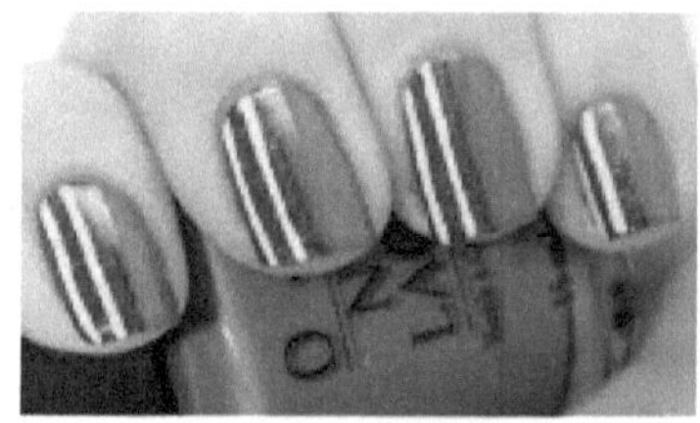

Materials

- Nail varnish in red, white and blue
- A cotton bud
- Nail varnish remover
- Cello tape

Directions

1. Start with clean nails – remove any residue polish or grease. Keep the cotton bud and varnish remover on hand in case you make any mistakes. Cover half of each nail with cello tape lengthways. Paint the other half with your blue color and allow to dry before removing the cello tape.

2. Once completely dry, cover the blue half with cello tape and paint the other half white. Allow to dry before removing the cello tape. Now paint two thin stripes of red over the white section at regular intervals, use the picture above as a reference. Allow to dry. Finish off with a clear topcoat.

Craft 28: Patriotic Table Setting

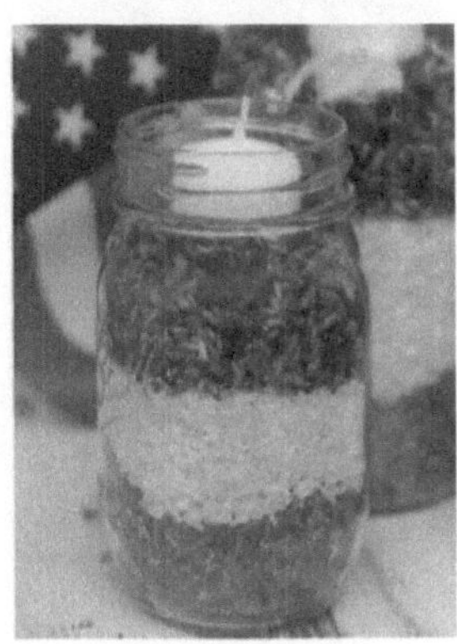

Materials

- Clear mason jars
- Enough rice to almost fill the mason jars
- Food coloring in red and blue
- Votive candles
- 3 Bowls

Directions

1. Divide the rice equally between the three bowls. To the first bowl, add some blue food coloring and mix well until all the rice is an even shade of blue. Set aside to dry. Repeat the process in the second bowl, this time using the red food coloring. The third bowl of rice will remain its normal color.

2. Line up your mason jars and pour a layer of red rice into each one. Follow with a layer of white rice and then red rice. Keep the layers as even as possible and leave a little space for the candle. Put your candles on top and you are ready to go.

Craft 29: Star Spangled Banner

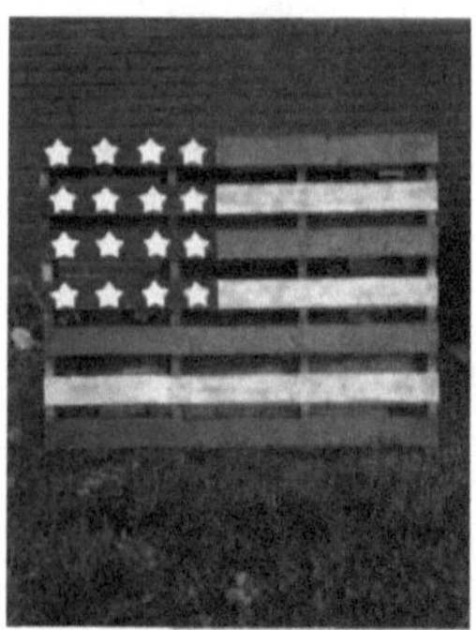

Materials

- A pallet
- Sandpaper
- Acrylic paint in red, white and blue
- Masking tape
- Paper or foam stars
- Scrap white paper
- Glue
- Wood sealant

Directions

1. Sand the pallet if necessary and wipe away all excess dust. Mask of the top left quarter of the banner to demarcate the blue rectangle on the flag. Mask off alternate stripes on the rest of the banner – every masked area of this section will remain white; the rest will be painted red. Paint the red stripes in and allow to dry.

2. Remove all the tape. Place your scrap paper around the outside edges of your rectangle and tape it to the white section of the stripes – this will allow you to paint in your blue without worrying about damaging the stripes. Set aside to dry. Glue on the stars and set aside to dry. Finish off with two coats of sealant, allowing each to dry before applying the next.

Craft 30: Patriotic Crib Blanket

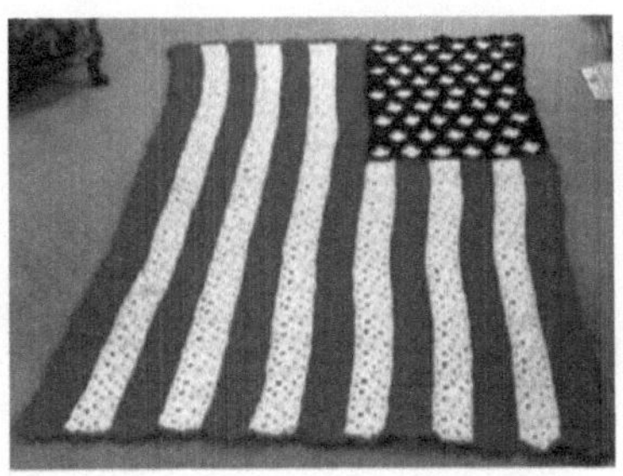

Materials

- Oddments of yarn in red, white and blue
- A crochet hook
- A yarn needle

Directions

1. Start by crocheting a granny square in the red yarn – 6 inches by 6 inches is a good size. Repeat using the blue yarn and the white yarn, making all the granny squares the same size. You need 54 squares in total – 18 of each color. Arrange the squares in rows of 6 across, one red, one white, one blue, etc. until all the squares have been used. Using leftover yarn, sew the squares together using invisible stitching.

Craft 31: Tissue Paper Votive

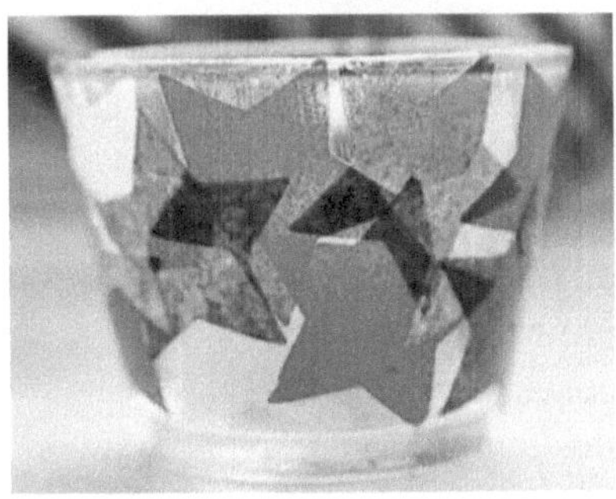

Materials

- Modge Podge
- Tissue Paper in red, white and blue

- Plain votive glasses
- A paint brush/sponge

Directions

1. Cut the tissue paper into stars – get a mix of colors. Set your votive glass upside down and plan where to place the first star – the stars will be on the outside of the glass. Glue the star in place with a little Modge Podge, taking care to smooth out any wrinkles.

2. Carry on adding stars until you have an effect that you like – overlap some of the edges but don't layer them too thickly or the colors will muddy. When you are happy with the effect, finish off with two layers of Modge Podge and set aside to dry.

Craft 32: Patriotic Glasses

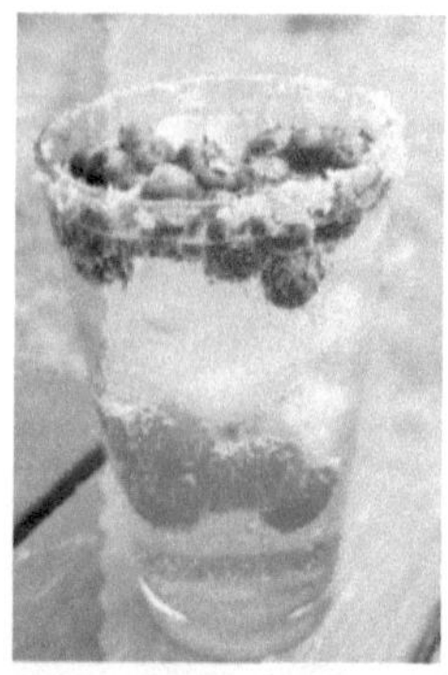

Materials

- Glasses
- Coarsely granulated sugar
- Food coloring in red and blue
- A freshly squeezed lemon
- Three side plates that the rim of the glass can fit into
- A spoon

Directions

1. This is one aspect of decoration that you can do a day or two in advance – it looks great and really doesn't require much effort at

all. You can, if you want to, also use plain sugar but don't go for sugar that is ground any finer than that. The larger the crystals here, the better. Divide the sugar between the three plates. One plate of sugar will be left as it is. Add a few drops of the red food coloring to the second and mix well. Then a few drops of the blue food coloring to the third plate of sugar and mix well.

2. Take the freshly squeezed lemon – you will be using the lemon itself here, keep the juice for something else – and run the cut edge around the rim of one of the glasses. Dunk the rim of the glass into one of the plates of sugar and twirl a little so that it is evenly coated. Repeat with the other glasses until you have decorated all of them. The little bit of lemon juice won't have much of an influence on the drink's flavor, if it has any but it is a great way to get the sugar to stick to the rim.

Craft 33: Easy Firework Prints

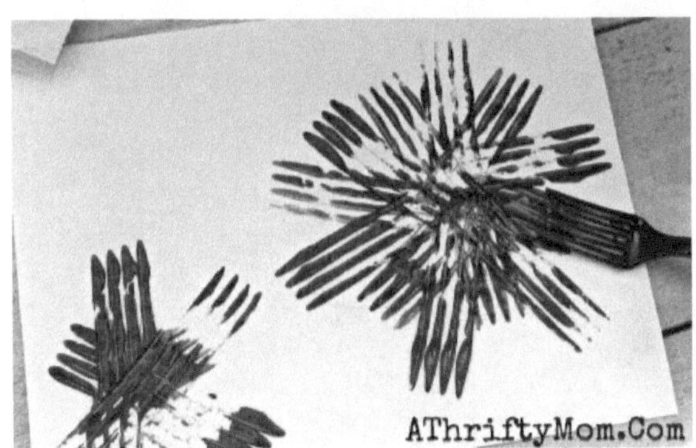

Materials

- Acrylic paint in red and white (metallic paint works really well)
- White paper
- Water
- 2 kitchen forks
- A couple of side plates

Directions

1. Decant a bit of red paint onto the side plate and add in a little water to make it more fluid. Coat the back of the fork prongs with the

paint and then immediately press onto the paper. The effect is the first burst of fireworks. Continue in this manner, rotating the page as you go to get the full effect. You can also, if you like drag the prongs a bit to get a longer burst of fireworks. Repeat with the blue paint until you have the look you want.

Craft 34: 4th of July Party Invitation Card

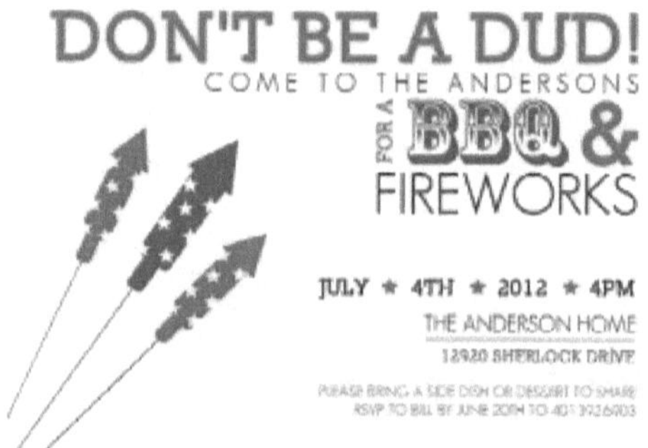

Materials

- A blank card
- Colored pencils
- Pens
- A template downloaded/clipart
- Glitter
- Glue

Directions

1. Google "Free 4th of July Printables" and you will find lots of graphics and cards that you can use. Alternatively draw your invitation free-hand. Decorate the card as you like – adding a little glitter and color to plain old clipart can be all that is required to take the invitation card from drab to fabulous.

Craft 35: 4th of July Costume

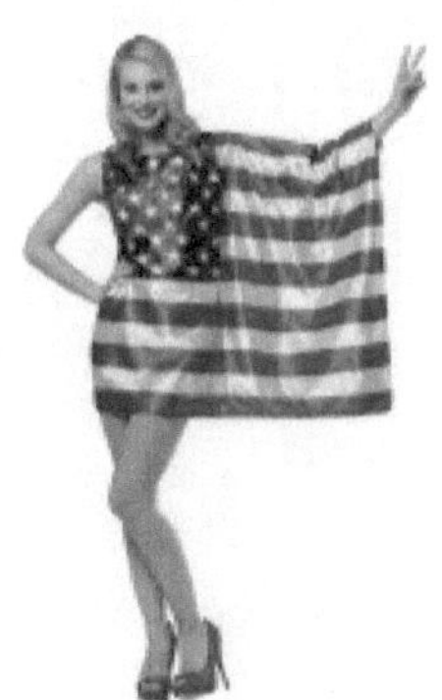

Materials

- Two pieces of fabric, preferably silk, with the imprint of American flag already on it.

Directions

1. With right sides facing, pin together the short sides at the edge of the fabric where the blue part of the flag starts, leaving about the top 6-7 inches open so that there is room for your arm to fit through. Sew the seam and press it open. Again, with right sides facing, pin the top of the flags together, leaving a gap about two inches from the star end of the fabric big enough for your head to fit through. The seam should extend to the end of this side of the fabric from the gap for your head. Sew the seam and press it open.

2. With the remaining side seam, mark out enough of a gap for your wrist and hand to comfortably fit through at the top of the seam. With right sides together, once again stitch the seam closed and press.

3. For the final seam, you need to measure your body at its widest point, add an inch and mark that distance on the last remaining open edge, starting from the left side where the stars are. Find the corresponding place on the top seam and mark that also. With right sides facing, sew the final seam, leaving the space marked open so that you can slip into your dress. Press. Turn the fabric right side out and, using a coordinating thread, topstitch a line from the bottom mark to the top mark, press and you are done.

Craft 36: Bottled Up

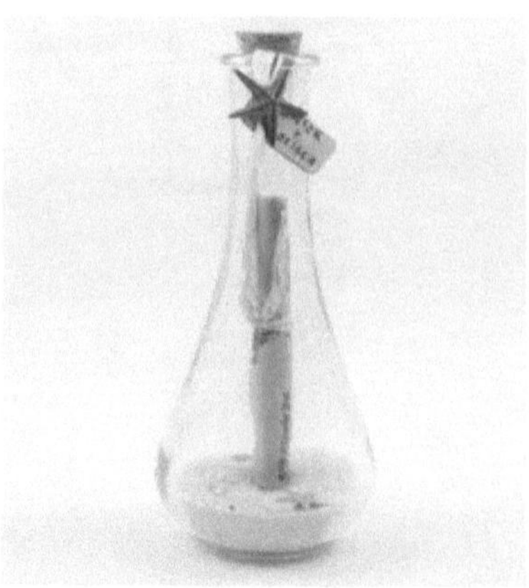

Materials

- Empty glass bottle
- Cork
- Paper
- Ribbon
- String
- Colored sand and tiny shells

Directions

1. Roll up a sheet of nice paper and make sure it fits in the bottle - cut it to size if not. Unroll and write your Mother's Day message on the paper. Re-roll it and tie a ribbon with a bow around it to stop it unraveling. Tie a length of string to the ribbon (not the bow) and tie the other end around the bottle cork. Put some colored sand and tiny shells into the bottle and then insert your rolled-up message. Put the cork in place. Finished!

Craft 37: The Layers of My Heart

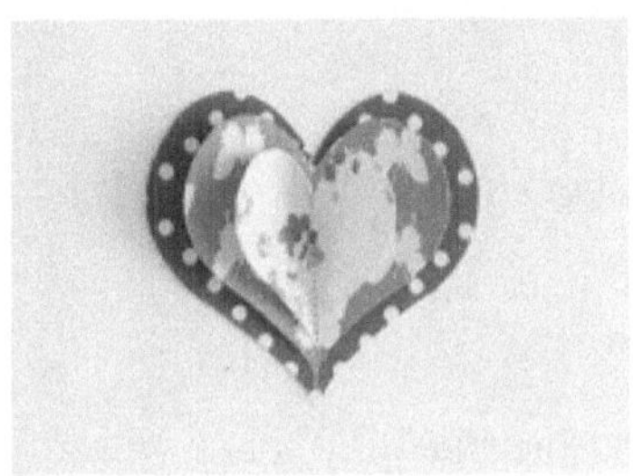

Materials

- Embossed card
- Hole puncher
- Silk ribbon
- Jewelry chain (optional)

Directions

1. Cut heart shapes from the card. Make each one the same size and shape. Use a hole punch to make holes in each heart and write a little message, or part of a message on each heart. Arrange the hearts in order, with the first message on the top, and thread the silk ribbon through the holes. Hold the layers in place by tying a knot before finishing the ribbon by tying a small bow. You can attach the pendant to a chain if you wish or allow your mom to do so herself.

Craft 38: You're the Key...

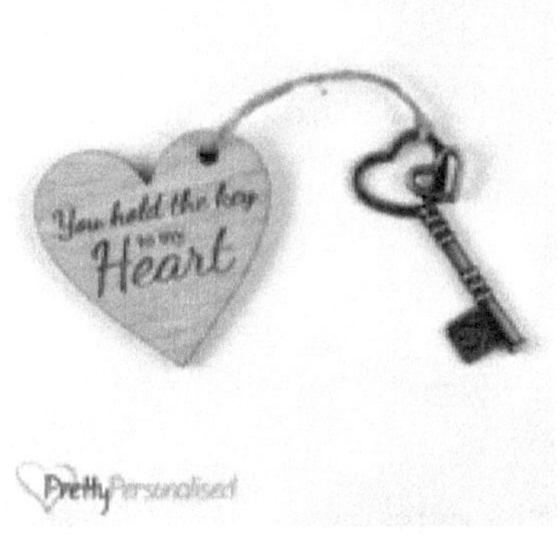

Materials

- Old key (the bigger the better)
- Card
- Ribbon
- Scissors
- Acrylic paint and brush (optional)

Directions

1. Clean the key and paint it if you wish. Allow to dry. Cut a heart shape from the card and on one side write: "Mom, you are". Turn the heart over and write: "My Life" (You don't need to write, "The key to" because the key says that for you!). Make a hole in the heart big enough to thread the ribbon through. Tie the ribbon to the key with a nice bow and wrap it appropriately.

Craft 39: Mom, You're No Mug!

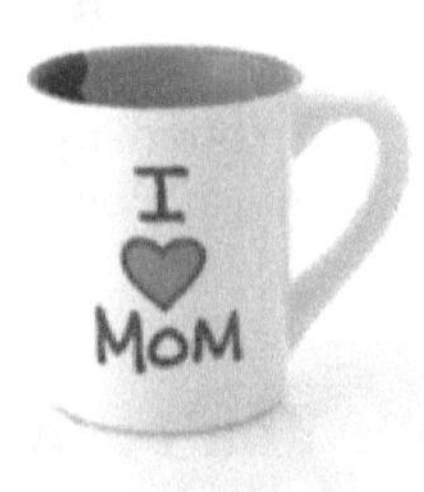

Materials

- Ceramic paint pen
- Plain white mug
- Oven

Directions

1. With the ceramic paint pen, write: "Mom's No Mug!" (Or any other message) on the mug and allow it to dry. It can take 24 hours.

Bake your "Mom's No Mug" mug in the oven for 30 minutes at 300 degrees to make it dishwasher safe.

Craft 40: Sweet Dreams Mommy

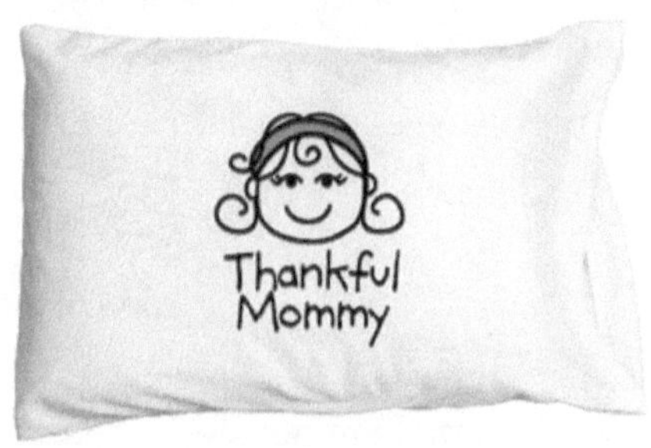

Materials

- Plain white pillowcase
- Pencil and paper
- Fabric markers
- Length of cardboard
- Clothes iron

Directions

1. Put the cardboard inside the pillowcase, pull it tight. (The cardboard stops the ink soaking through and makes the pillowcase easier to write on.). With the fabric marker write: "Sweet Dreams Mommy!" on the pillow case - practice on a piece of paper first so you don't end up having to squeeze it all in. Add any extra touches or flourishes you want to - hearts, flowers, even sheep! Make the message permanent by ironing the pillowcase.

Craft 41: Mother's Day Egg Cup

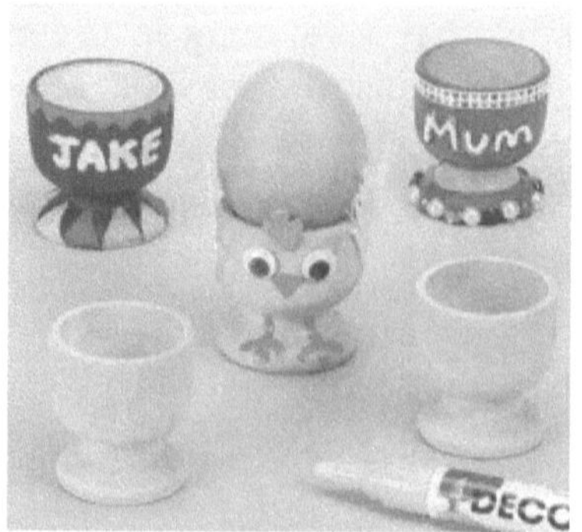

Materials

- Permanent or semi-permanent pens
- Acrylic paint and paint brush
- Wooden egg cup (empty)
- Acrylic varnish (optional)
- Stickers or cut outs (optional)

Directions

1. Coat the egg cup with acrylic paint and leave it to dry. Next, write a short personal message or simply "Mum" or "Mother" and draw on some flowers. To beautify the egg cup and make it extra special, use a small paintbrush and acrylic paint for flourishes. You could even use some tiny cut-outs from wrapping paper or stickers using white (PVA) glue. Just apply some acrylic varnish to shield the egg cup and make your design last longer.

Craft 42: Mother's Day Candle

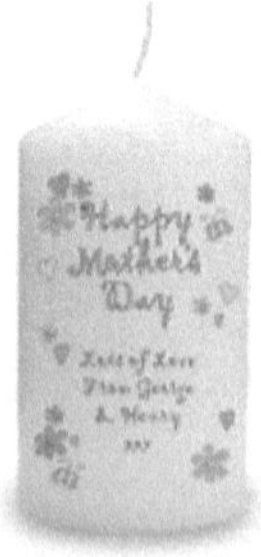

Materials

- Wooden spoon
- Heatproof bowl
- Plain candle
- Large pan
- Crayons
- Paintbrushes

Directions

1. Fill one third of the pan with water and put it on a gentle heat. Place the bowl in the pan in such a way that it doesn't touch the bottom of the pan. Remove the paper from a crayon, put half of it into the bowl and mix with the wooden spoon until it melts.

2. Take the bowl out of the pan and place it on something that is heatproof. Now you're ready to paint the candle with the melted colored crayon wax - take care because both the bowl and wax will be hot. Use an old brush to paint on your design or message. Rinse out the bowl and melt another color crayon to add come variation to your candle. Use a different brush for each color because you will find that the brushes get hard after using once. This craft should be supervised by an adult and candles must be lit by adults!

Craft 43: "I Love..." Flower

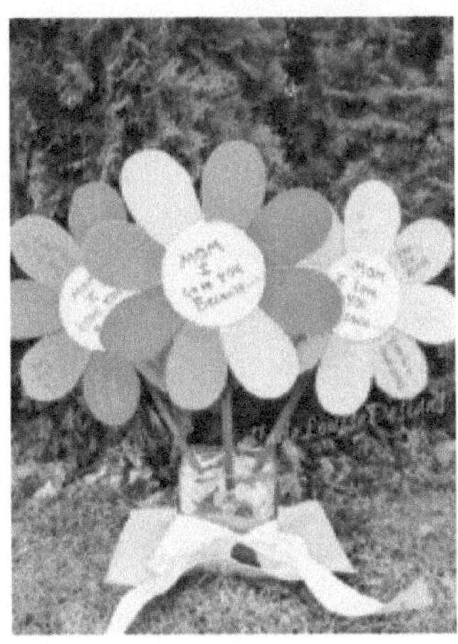

Materials

- Scissors
- Pens
- Colored card
- Glue
- Drinking straw (optional)

Directions

1. Sketch a circle and draw six petals on the card. In the center of the circle write 'I love my sweet Mum because…'. On each petal, write a message or draw a reason why you love your mother. Be imaginative and make it personal. Cut your flower petals and the circle out with the scissors. Glue the petals to the circle and leave for a while to dry. Now you can attach your flower to a card for a beautiful Mother's Day card, or attach a drinking straw to the back and pop it in a (self-made) vase.

Craft 44: Foam Vase

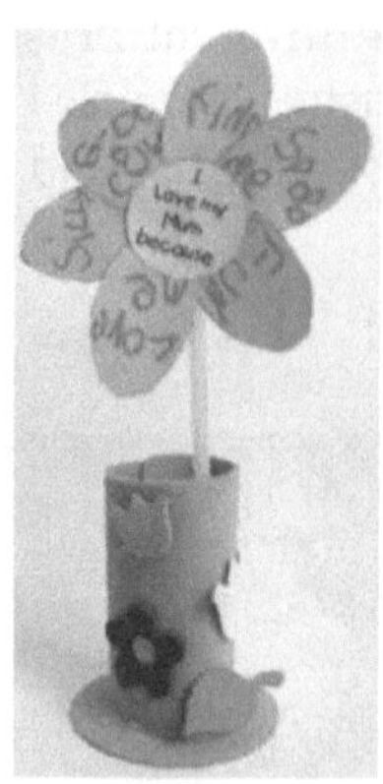

Materials

- Glue
- Double sided sticky tape
- Craft foam flowers or other embellishments
- Craft foam

Directions

1. Sketch around a cup to draw a circle on the craft foam and use the scissors to cut it out. Next, cut a rectangle of about 10cm by 15cm from the craft foam. Roll it to make a tube and use the double sided sticky tape to fix the sides together. Cover one end of the tube with glue and place it on the center of the circle. Attach the foam flowers on to the vase and leave it to dry.

Craft 45: Heart Plaque Key Ring

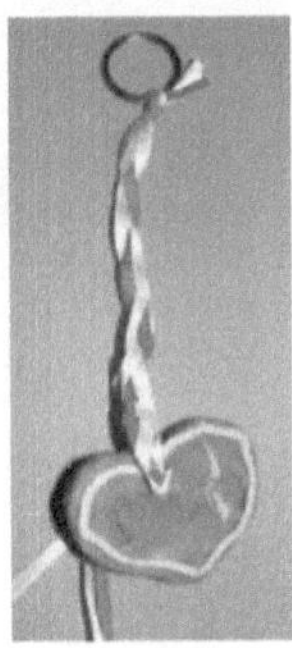

Materials

- Three shades of thin ribbon
- Heart-shaped cookie cutter (optional)
- Polymer clay
- Key ring fitting/hoop (optional)

Directions

1. Roll out your clay and using a heart-shaped template or cookie cutter, make a heart shape from the clay. (If you haven't got a heart shape cutter, use a knife to cut out a heart.). Embellish your heart with other colors of clay or make patterns with modeling tools. With a toothpick make a hole through the top of the heart - wiggle it around so the hole will be big enough to thread the ribbon through after the clay has baked.

2. Heat the heart following the manufacturer's instructions. While it's 'cooking', group your ribbons together like a ponytail, knot and tie them together. When the heart has cooled down, thread the ribbons

through the hole and tie a knot on either side to secure it in position. Leave an inch or so of ribbon hanging untied. If you want to put the heart on a purse, pencil case or a bag, you can tie the ribbons onto a key ring fitting/hoop and use that to attach it to the bag's zipper.

Craft 46: Heart Fridge Magnet

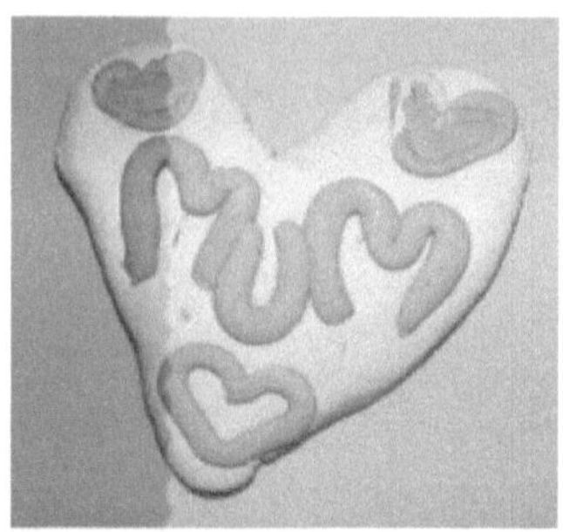

Materials

- Strong glue
- A magnet back (available from craft shops)
- Two colors of polymer clay
- Heart cookie cutter (optional)

Directions

1. Roll out one color of clay, and cut a heart shape - you can do this with a shaped cookie cutter or knife. Roll out the other color clay and make a long, thin sausage shape. This roll will form your letters so cut a length and shape them to spell Mom/Mum or other initials that you like. Arrange these onto the heart and press gently into place.

2. Use any leftover clay from the 'sausage' to decorate - shape one or two heart outlines, a star or simple flower. Harden it with heat as said by the manufacturer's instructions. When it's cooled down, attach the magnet to the back with glue.

Craft 47: Heart Felt Pillow

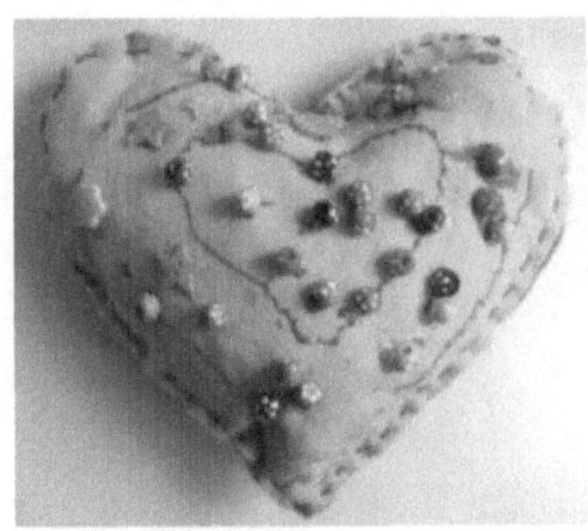

Materials

- Fabric scraps (for pillow stuffing)
- Needle and thread
- Beads, sequins, fabric paint (to decorate)
- Fabric glue
- 2 sheets of felt in pink or red
- Scissors

Directions

1. Cut two big hearts from the felt. Beautify both the hearts with anything suitable from your craft cupboard - beads, sequins or simply use fabric paint to personalize it. You might choose to decorate only one of the hearts or might go for an all over design. Sew the two hearts together when the glue and fabric paint have dried. Remember to leave a gap big enough to stuff the pillow - you can use fabric scraps or stuffing from old toys or pillows.

2. Tidy the gap when make sure the stuffing doesn't come out by making some small holes in the felt and threading through a nice ribbon before tying securely. You can make a loop to hang the pillow if you wish.

Craft 48: Daisy Picture

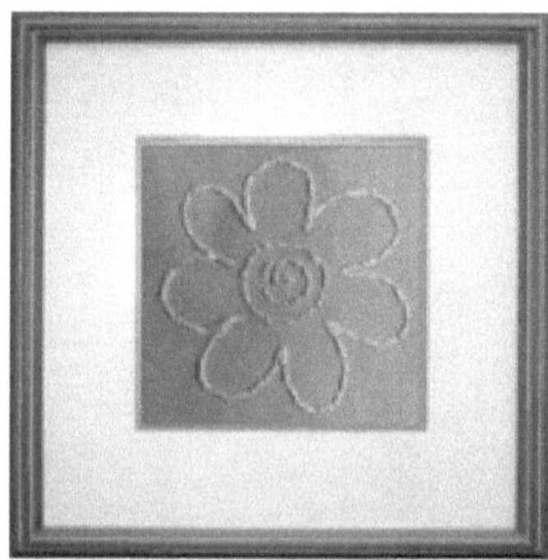

Materials

- Needle with large eye (blunt for younger children)
- Green card
- White and yellow embroidery thread or yarn
- Pencil
- Tea towel

Directions

1. Draw an outline of the flower on the back of the card. Place the card on the tea towel, and going along the outline you have drawn, punch holes with your needle - space them evenly and make enough. Thread the needle and tie one end to the back of the card, and begin to embroider your design. You can cut the daisy out and glue it onto another card, or frame the picture for a special Mother's Day gift...or any other occasion!

Craft 49: Red Rose Filter

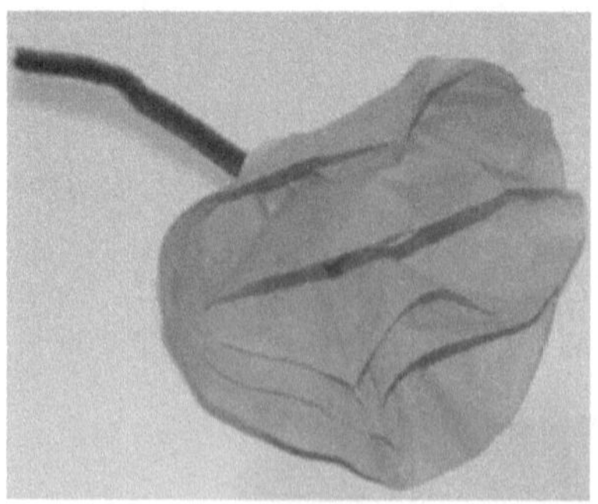

Materials

- Green chenille stem
- Red paint and water
- 3 coffee filter papers
- Scissors

Directions

1. Dilute and thin the paint with water and then coat the filter papers and allow to dry. Trim two of the filter papers so that you have three different sizes by cutting around the edges. Fix the smaller two papers inside the largest one. Stretch out into a cone shape and twirl the bottom to form a point. Hold the papers together by wrapping one end of the chenille stem around the point, leaving the other end as it is to make the flower's stem.

Craft 50: Bath Salts

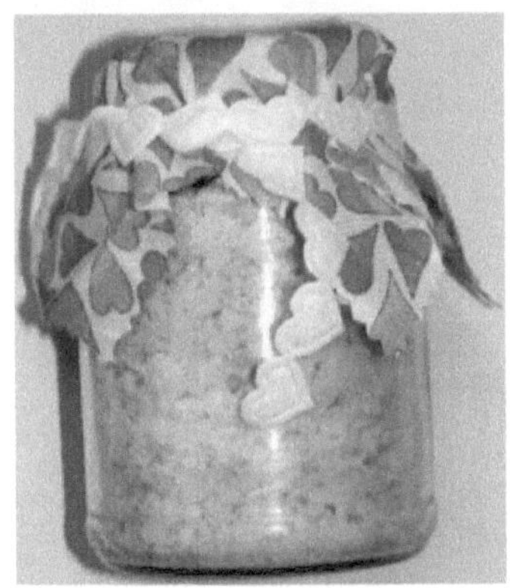

Materials

- Pretty fabric ribbon
- Glass jar
- Essential oil
- Food coloring (powder or paste, not liquid)
- Plain bath salts
- Mixing bowl and spoon

Directions

1. Mix some the plain bath salts, small amount of food coloring and just a couple of drops of essential oil in the bowl. Mix them well until all of the salts soak up the color. You can repeat the process with as many different colors as you like. Pour the salts carefully into a clean jar layering with different colors. Cut a piece of fabric to fit over the top of the jar and tie it up with some pretty ribbon.

Craft 51: Decoupage Tray Photo Frame

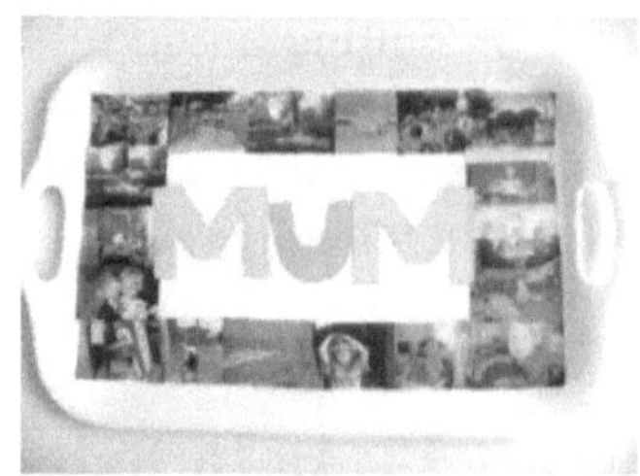

Materials

- Photos
- Acrylic varnish
- Glue
- Colored paper
- Photos
- Emulsion paint (if required)
- An old or inexpensive tray
- Scissors

Directions

1. If required, freshen the tray with a coat or two of emulsion paint. Position your photos and when you're happy with the look of the tray, fix them carefully with glue. Cut letters from colored paper to spell 'mum/mom,' arrange and glue these to the tray. To seal any loose edges paint over the letters with a layer of glue and then leave the tray to dry. Finally, paint a layer of acrylic varnish to give the tray an extra level of protection - be careful not to paint the photos!

Craft 52: Handprint Heart Card

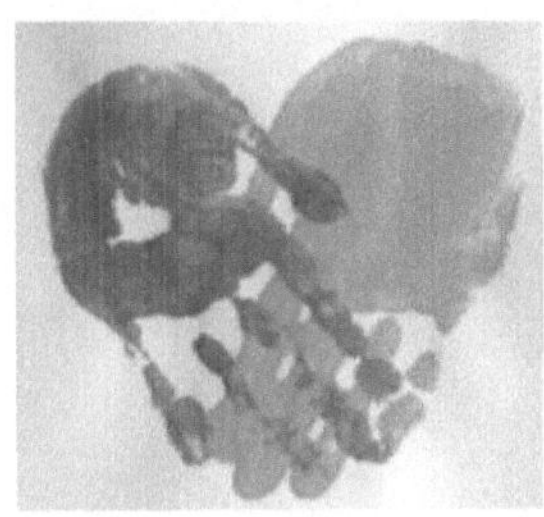

Materials

- Card and newspaper
- Pink and purple paint
- Two trays or paint brush

Directions

1. Practice makes perfect so use newspaper first to experiment with before printing your card. Fold the card in half to make a greeting card. With the purple paint, cover the palm of your hand with a brush or dip it in a tray and then carefully make a handprint on the center of the paper. Use your other hand and make a handprint with the pink paint to create a beautiful and simple handprint card. Or - instead of a card, you can make a great picture by adding extra handprints and framing the card.

Craft 53: Key Ring Purse

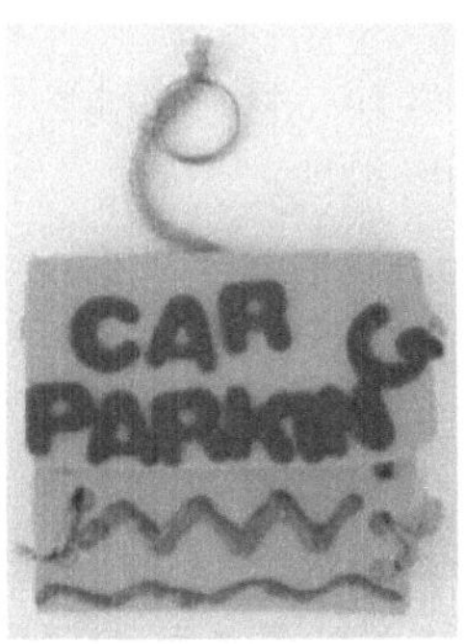

Materials

- Craft foam
- Key ring fitting/hoop (from craft shops)
- Yarn (wool)
- Hole punch or darning needle
- Fabric paint, foam stickers, other embellishments
- Eye fasteners and self-adhesive hook

Directions

1. Cut the craft foam into a rectangle, with the long edges being the sides. Fold the rectangle so that the bottom edge is about an inch from the top. Fold the top edge over it to create the shape of your purse. Sew the sides with a darning needle, making some punch holes first to ease the sewing. Secure both ends of the thread with a knot. Fasten the top flap with an eye fastener and a hook. Make two tiny holes in the top of the purse and thread through a length of yarn. Knot the ends together, tying the key ring fitting/hoop. Have some fun embellishing your purse by drawing or painting on some designs or by writing a personal message.

Craft 54: Charming Bracelet

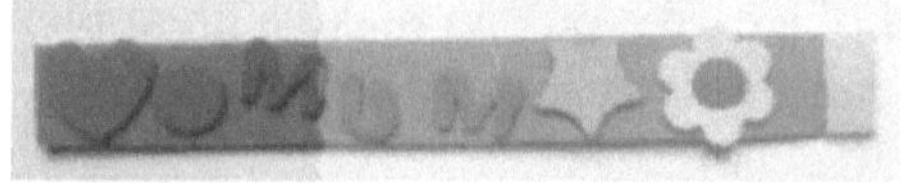

Materials

- Foam stickers (letters, flowers and hearts) or other embellishments
- Hook and eye fasteners
- Craft foam
- Scissors

Directions

1. Cut a rectangle from the craft foam, one-inch wide and long enough to go around Mother's wrist (with an extra inch to spare). You can also cut the edges of the rectangle into a pattern to make the bracelet extra special! Attach the eye fastening to one end of

the bracelet, and the hook fastening to the other end to make the bracelet. Adorn the bracelet with the foam stickers or other embellishments.

Craft 55: Charcoal Canvas Sketch

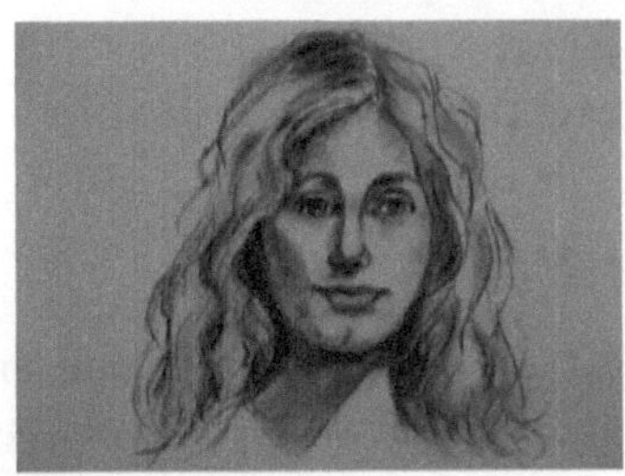

Materials

- Photocopy of a photo of Mom (or get her to pose for you!)
- Paints and brushes (whatever type you are comfortable using)
- Stretched canvas
- Charcoal stick

Directions

1. With the charcoal, trace over all the details on the photocopy of the photo. Put the photocopy face down on the canvas and rub the back of the paper to transfer the image. Carefully lift the paper from the canvas and paint in the colors you wish. Use bright, complementary colors for a cheerful, vibrant picture. Older children might add a realistic background and younger ones a more abstract block color design.

Craft 56: Handprint Magnets

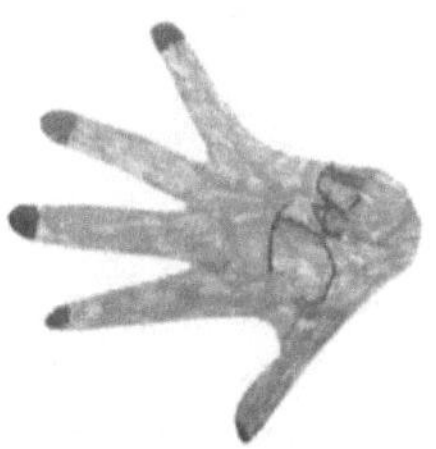

Materials

- Laminator
- Strong glue
- Craft magnets
- White card
- Scissors
- Poster paint, felt-tip pens, crayons or coloring pencils

Directions

1. Help your kid to trace around their hand onto white card. Prettify the 'hand' using felt-tip pens, crayons, pencils or paints in whatever way you like - a nice touch is to write a name on the front and date on the back. Cut out the 'hand' and laminate the card. Trim the laminate leaving an approximately half inch border around the hand. Use strong glue to fix a magnet to the back of the hand.

Craft 57: Painted Flower Pots

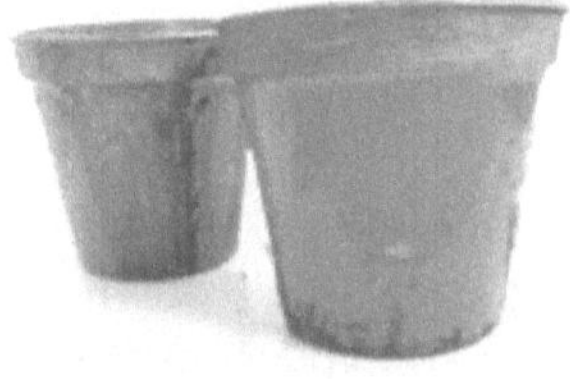

Materials

- Plastic or terracotta plant pots
- Acrylic paints and brushes
- Painter's tape
- Acrylic varnish (optional)

Directions

1. Stick tape to the pots to make a stencil on one side - simple lines are so effective! Paint over the taped side of the pot, and on the other side paint a pretty flower, star, heart or something else that's really personal. When the paint's dry, peel away the tape and

expose your stripes. To make the painted pot more weather proof, brush on a coat of acrylic varnish.

Craft 58: Paper Mache Bowl

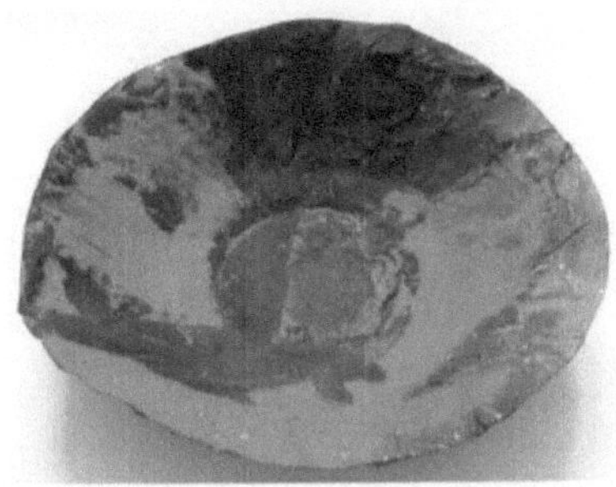

Materials

- Acrylic varnish
- Acrylic paints
- PVA glue
- Strips of newspaper
- White paper towels
- Food wrap (cling film)
- Bowl to use as a mold

Directions

1. Turn your bowl upside down and cover it with food wrap. Mix some water with glue. Cover your strips of paper with the glue, dipping them into the mix one at a time and start sticking them to the bowl. After covering the whole bowl with paper strips, leave it to dry. Repeat the process with a second and a third layer - allow the layer to dry before adding another. For the final layer, use strips of white paper towel instead of newspaper which will make the painting easier and better.

2. When the paper is dry, remove your new bowl carefully and peel off the food wrap. Now, tidy and trim the edges by carefully cutting and gluing any fraying. Or, you can form a rim by wrapping more short strips over the edge. When it's completely dry,

paint your bowl with acrylic paint. Allow to dry again and add a coat of acrylic varnish for extra protection.

Craft 59: Photo Coaster

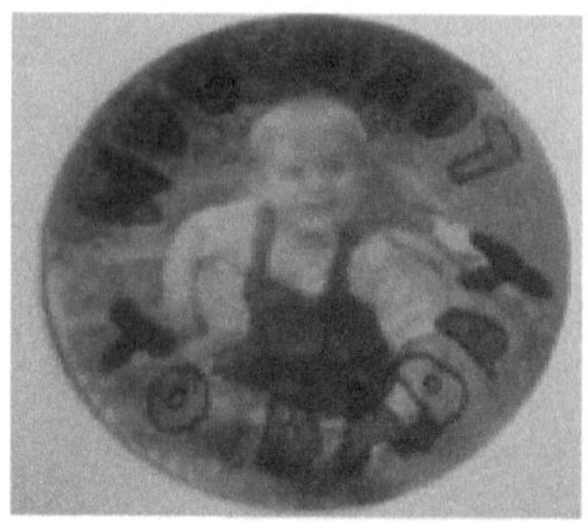

Materials

- Laminated photo
- Permanent marker pens
- CD/DVD
- Scissors or craft knife
- Super glue
- PVA glue or acrylic varnish (optional)

Directions

1. Before laminating the photo, cut it to the same size as the CD/DVD and write a message on it using permanent markers. Cut the laminated photo and then use super glue to fix it to the printed side of the disc. To seal, smother the edge with PVA glue or acrylic varnish and leave it to dry.

Craft 60: Ribbon Bracelet

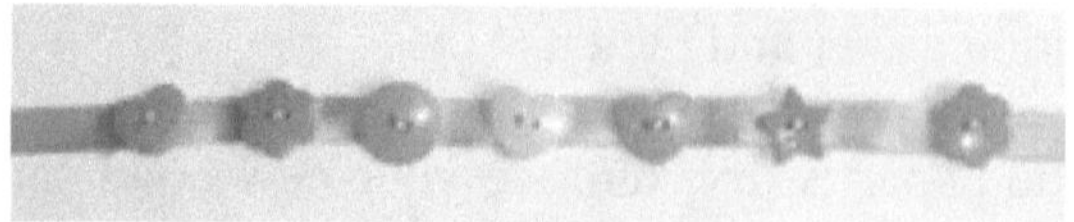

Materials

- Pretty buttons

- Ribbon
- Needle and thread

Directions

1. Cut a length of ribbon that's long enough to wrap around your mother's wrist, with four inches to spare. Leave about two-and-half inches of ribbon free at both end and sew your buttons along the ribbon. Your bracelet is now ready to wear!

Craft 61: Finger Print Photo Frame

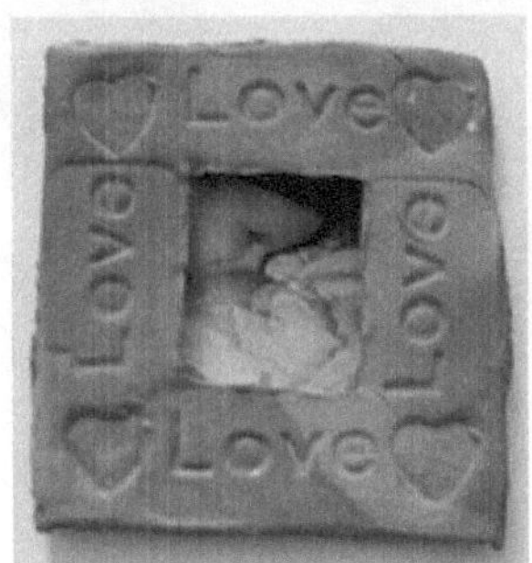

Materials

- Colored air (hardening clay)
- Photo
- Card
- Pencil (optional)
- Double sided sticky tape
- Acrylic paint (optional)

Directions

1. Roll out your clay and cut the shape of the frame according to your preferred size. Place the photo on top and measure before cutting and carefully removing the middle to leave you with the just the edges of the frame. Now gently push your fingerprint into the clay. Going around the edge. You can also use a pencil to write on a message by 'engraving' the letters with its nib.

2. Leave your frame to harden - this may take a couple of days. When the clay has hardened, use acrylic paint to color if you wish. Cut a piece of card that's just slightly smaller than the frame and use double sided sticky tape to fix it on the back. Next, turn the frame over. Place some tape in the corners of your photo and stick it onto the card.

Craft 62: Simple Silhouettes

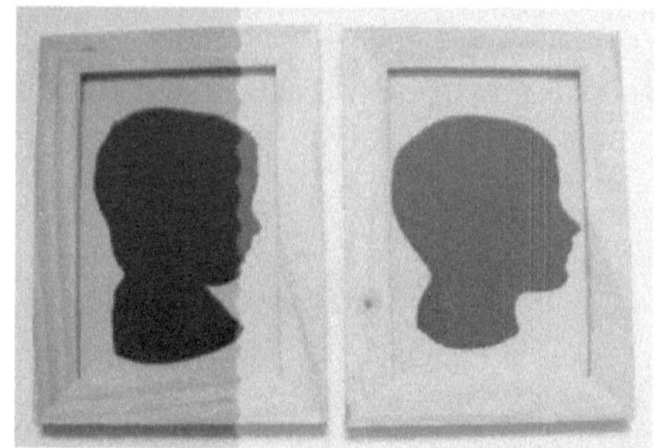

Materials

- Picture frame
- Backing card
- A dark shade of card
- Glue stick
- A profile photo (printed on standard paper will be fine)

Directions

1. Cut a piece of backing card that will fit your photo frame. Paste your photo onto the dark card. Carefully cut around the profile of the photo. At the neck, cut a curve to achieve a traditional silhouette profile or leave it straight for a more modern look. Use the glue stick to fix the silhouette cut-out onto the backing card - remember the photo will be face down. Frame your silhouette!

Craft 63: Kangaroo and Joey

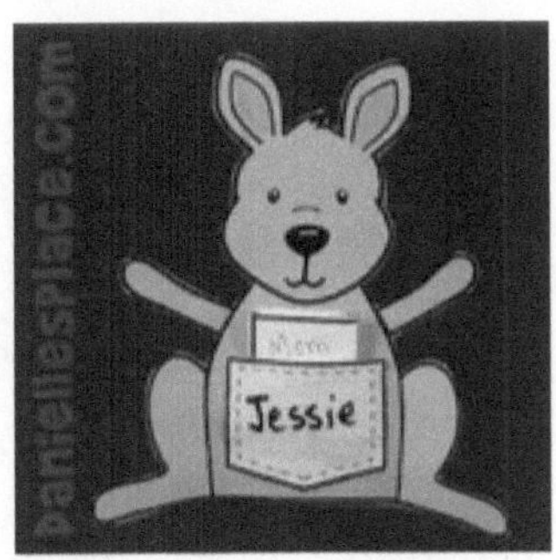

Materials

- Card
- Pictures of a kangaroo and joey
- Pencil
- Colored markers
- Paper
- Stapler
- Craft knife
- Scissors

Directions

1. Put the picture of the kangaroo and joey onto the card. Use a pencil and some pressure to draw around the shape to make an indent on the card. Remove the pictures and trace over the indented lines to make them visible. You can color them in with markers and add other details. Next, make a slice with the craft knife where the kangaroo's pocket is. Cut out the kangaroo and joey.

2. Write a nice Mother's Day message on a piece of paper and fold so that it can slide into the kangaroo's pocket. Leave a little bit sticking out of the top and write 'To Mom' on it. Arrange the kangaroo and joey on another piece of card and when you're happy with their position, glue them in place. Be careful with the glue so that you don't stick the message to the card or kangaroo!

Craft 64: Say It with Flowers

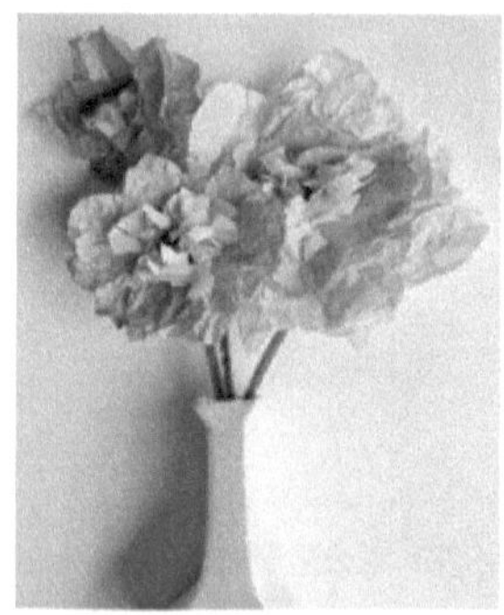

Materials

- Tissue paper
- Sequins, buttons or beads (for the center of the flower)
- Chenille stems
- Ribbon
- Scissors
- Glue

Directions

1. Cut flower shapes from the animal print tissue paper. To make the flower, you need to cut each shape a little smaller than the previous one. Ruffle the tissue to shape the flower and then fix them together by putting a dab of glue in the center of each and then placing them one on top of the other - start with the biggest flower on the bottom, and work your way up.

2. Open the flower head and glue a button, bead, or sequin in the center of the flower. Attach a chenille stem to the back of the flower head for the stem. When you have made enough for a small bouquet tie them together with a ribbon finished off with a bow.

Craft 65: Read Me, Plant Me, Feed Me!

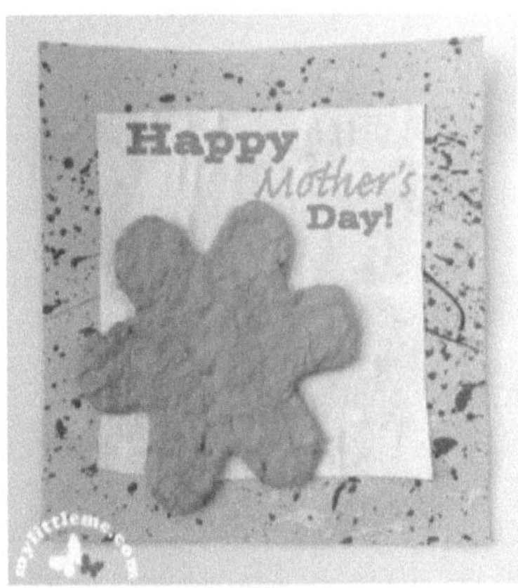

Materials

- Handmade seed paper
- Pens

Directions

1. All you need for to make this really brilliant Mother's Day card is handmade seed paper. Fold the seed paper to regular card size. Write your message on the front - 'Read Me, Plant Me, Feed Me!' and add a drawing of a flower or whatever else you like. Don't forget to tell your mom that after reading the card, she has to tear it then plant it for the seeds to grow into beautiful flowers. To make sure they do, feed them with regular water!

Craft 66: Mommy Bear Wiggle-Jiggle

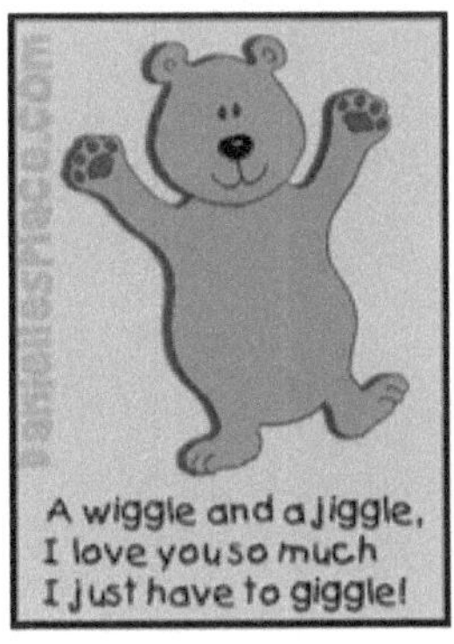

Materials

- Card
- Pictures of a mommy bear
- Glue
- Tape
- Scissors
- Crayons or colored pencils
- Cardstocks

Directions

1. Glue the picture of the mommy bear onto card - or draw your own. Cut around it carefully - if you've drawn the bear color it in first and then cut around it. To make it jiggle and wiggle, cut a thin strip of card and very gently roll it so that it's loose when you unroll it. Glue one end of the roll to a new piece of card. Allow the glue to dry, and gently re-roll the thin strip, keeping it loose. Put some glue on the roll and gently the bear into position. Allow the glue to dry and then pick up the card to see mommy bear wiggle and jiggle!

Craft 67: Cupcake Sweetie

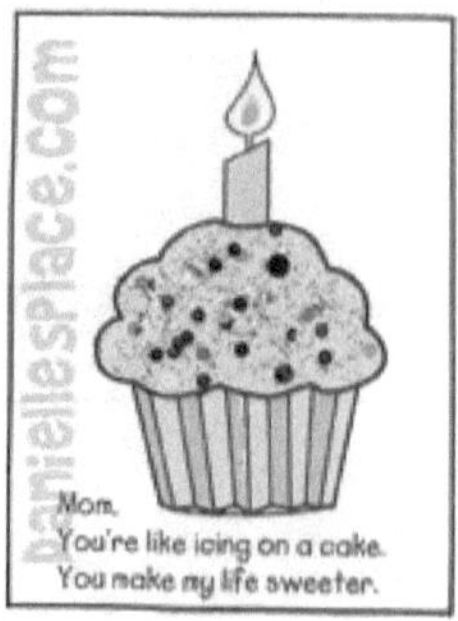

Materials

- Card
- Sequins and other decorative items
- Glue
- Crayons and pens

Directions

1. Draw a picture of a cup cake on a card and color it with crayons, leaving space at the top and bottom to write your message. Apply some sparkle and texture by gluing glitter and sequins onto the cupcake and allow to dry. Now write your message. At the top write: "Mom, you're the icing on a cup cake...". At the bottom write: "Because you make my life sweeter!"

Craft 68: You Make Me Whole!

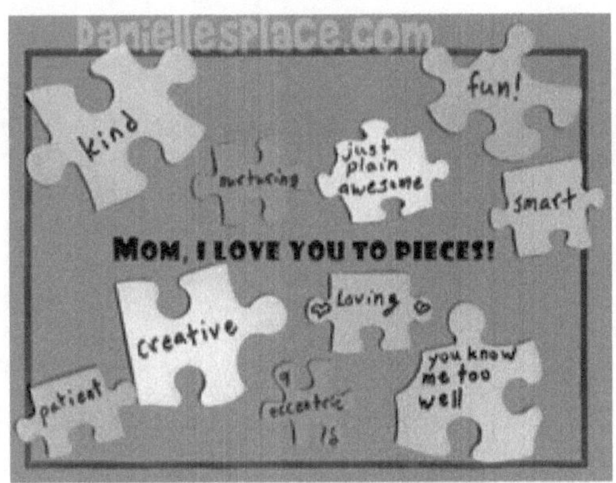

Materials

- Craft foam
- Scissors (or craft knife)
- Permanent markers
- Envelope or gift bag

Directions

1. Draw simple jigsaw shapes on the craft foam. Next, write - Mom, You Make Me Whole! - In big letters on the craft foam using permanent markers. Draw any other details you wish - hearts, stars, or other words in different colors. Cut the craft foam into simple jigsaw shapes. Place them all in an envelope or a fancy gift bag.

Craft 69: Mom, You're Beary Special!

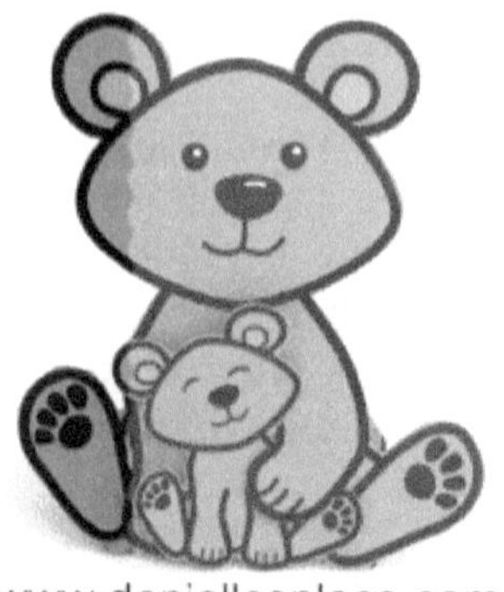

www.daniellesplace.com

Materials

- Cardstock
- Colored pencils
- Scissors

Directions

1. Draw and color a mommy bear and a baby bear on the card. (The mommy bear's arm needs to be drawn in a way that it will wrap around and cuddle the baby bear.). Cut the bears out with scissors. Make a cut around mommy bear's arm and hand so that you can slide baby bear under it. Take baby bear out and write on the big bear's belly, "Mom, You're Beary Special!" so that it isn't noticeable when baby is back in her arms. Glue mommy to a big card and when it's dry and slide baby back under her under arm.

Craft 70: Pebble Portrait - "Mom, You Rock!"

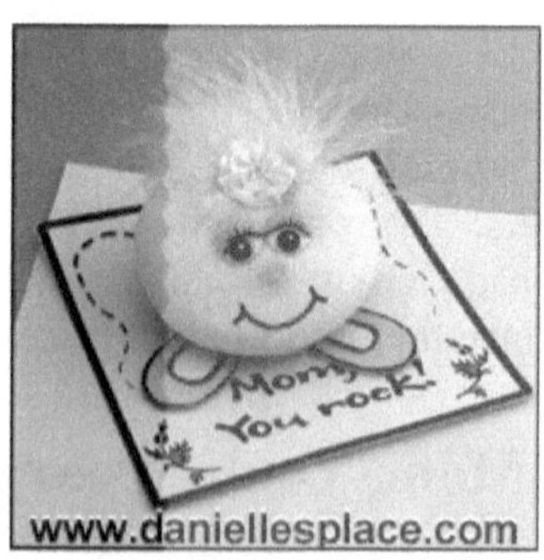

www.daniellesplace.com

Materials

- Smooth pebble
- Wiggle eyes
- Wool (for hair)
- Acrylic paint and brushes
- Glue
- Card
- Permanent markers
- Small box (to fit the pebble)

Directions

1. Clean the pebble and paint on a face. When the paint is dry add some fun and an extra dimension by gluing on wiggle eyes and using wool for the hair. Cut the card to fit the top of the small box and write "Mom, You Rock" on it. Glue it to the box and insert your pebble portrait.

Craft 71: "Mom...You're Purrfect!"

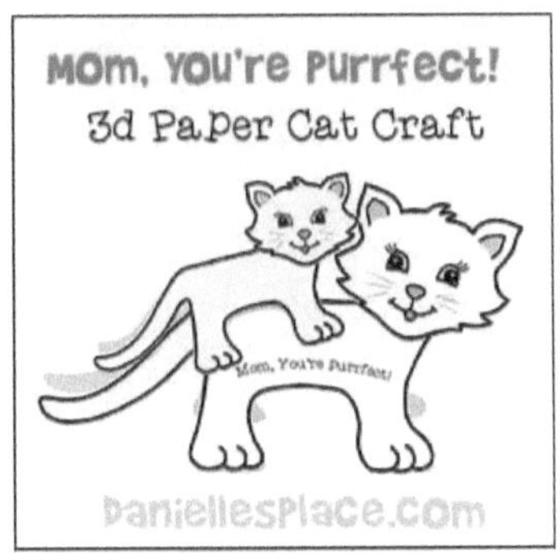

Materials

- Card
- Picture of a cat and kitten
- Photo of mom and you
- Tape
- Scissors
- Colored pencil

1. Glue the cat and kitten pictures to the card, or draw and color your own. Carefully use the scissors to cut around the cats. Now for mom, so take even more care with her photo! Cut around her head and yours, using a soft curve at the neck. Glue the big cat onto the card and glue the kitten onto its back. Now, glue your face on the kitten, and your mom's onto the cat. At the top of the card, above the cats write: "The 2 of Us are just...". And underneath the cats write: "PURRFECT!"

Craft 72: Message on A Candle

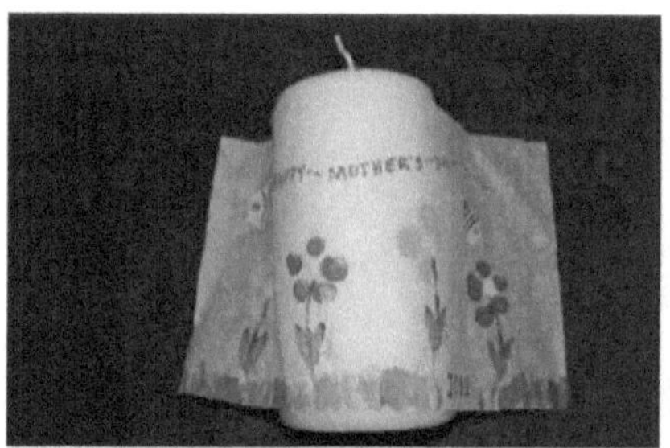

Materials

- White tissue paper
- Markers
- Scissors
- White pillar candles
- Parchment or waxed paper
- Hair dryer

Directions

1. Wrap the candle with the tissue paper and cut it to fit. Remove the tissue paper and using the markers, draw your designs and write your Mother's Day message. Tissue paper is delicate - practice!

2. Rewrap the candle with the tissue paper and then wrap that with your waxed paper or parchment. Now use the hairdryer to transfer the design onto the candle - use the high heat setting and hold it close. The tissue paper will slowly disappear - when it's no longer

visible you can stop. Carefully unwrap the waxed paper to reveal your unique Mother's Day candle - a beautiful gift she's sure to adore!

Craft 73: Bath Bomb for Mom!

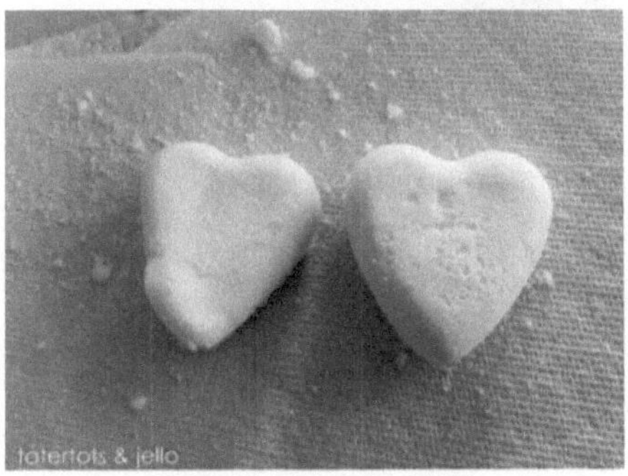

Materials

- 2 cups of bicarbonate/baking soda
- 1-2 table spoons of olive oil
- Food coloring
- 1 cup cream of tartar
- Water in a spray bottle
- Silicone ice cube tray

Directions

1. Mix all the ingredients well until you are happy with the color. Give it 2-3 sprays of water and start mixing until it feels a bit like wet sand (the water will make the baking soda fizz). When you can make a good indent and shape with a spoon without it crumbling, the mix is ready. Transfer it into the silicone ice cube trays (other trays work but it's very hard to remove your 'bombs' without them breaking). Press the mix down hard and let them dry and harden - one or two days.

2. When they are set, gently remove the 'bombs' and put them into nice bags. If they break apart when you remove them from the tray, don't panic - simply crumble it all up again, spray a little on water, remix and try again.

Craft 74: Rustic Photo Frame

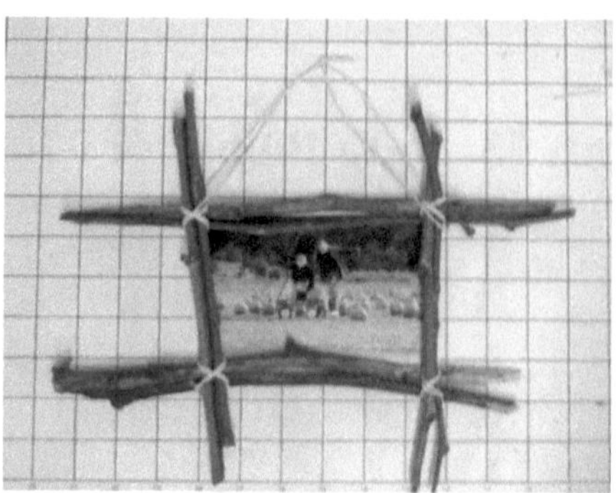

Materials

- Twigs
- Wooden picture frame
- Hot glue and gun
- Family photo

Directions

1. Gather your twigs and measure them with the picture frame's border and then break them to size. You can arrange them vertically, horizontally, diagonally. Apply hot glue to the frame and attach the twigs. Continue until the whole frame is covered. Put your family photo inside the frame - your mom will be thrilled!

Craft 75: Sugar Scrub Pamper

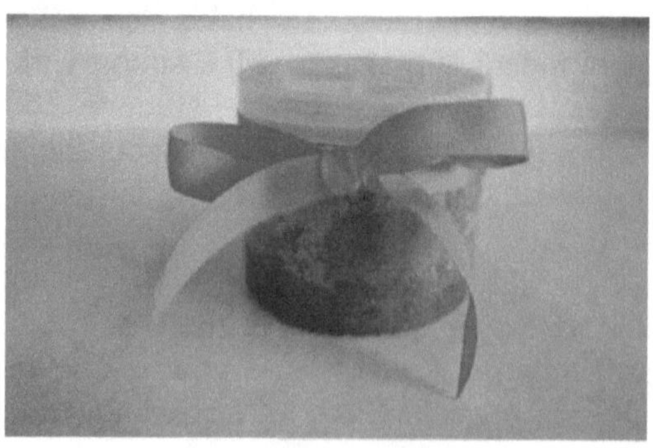

Materials

- Sugar
- Olive oil
- Essential oils (e.g. lavender, jasmine, vanilla)
- Food coloring
- Mixing bowl
- Jar with a top
- Ribbon

Directions

1. Mix the ingredients - 3 cups of white sugar, 1 cup and 2 tbsp. of olive oil, 10 (or more) drops of essential oil and a few drops of food coloring (just a little to tint the scrub - you don't want to end up dying your skin!). When the ingredients have been well mixed, pack the sugar scrub into your jar. Add a special touch by tying the ribbon around it or add a personalized Mother's Day sticker.

Craft 76: Celebrate with Personalized Glasses

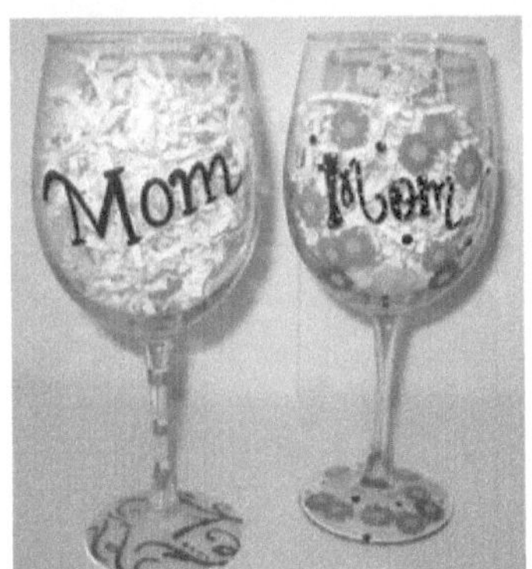

Materials

- Drinking glasses
- Paint brushes
- Glass paint
- Oven and baking sheet

1. Make sure your glasses are clean and dry before you start. Choose your colors and paint on your Mother's Day message, your mom's name or anything you want to. For stronger colors, add layers but wait for each coat to dry before painting a new one. Place the glasses on a baking tray and put them in a cold oven. Turn the oven up to 350 degrees or its maximum heat and leave the glasses in there for 30 minutes. Let the glasses cool before taking them out - they're now dishwasher safe and ready for use! Cheers and Happy Mother's Day!

Craft 77: Mustache Mug

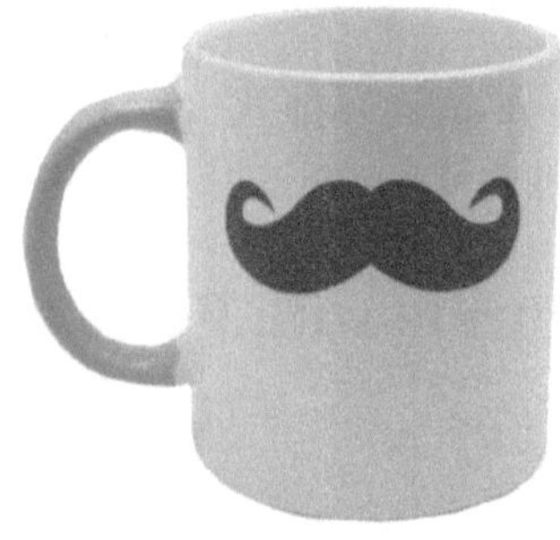

Materials

- Mug
- Paper
- Tape
- Nail polish (paint)
- Marker

Directions

1. Select a mug that is clean and that has no writings on it or any other form of patterns. Take the paper and use the marker or pencil to draw a mustache that is proportional to the size of the mug. The right size of the mustache will make it more effective.

2. After you are done drawing, cut out the mustache and leave the empty space. Make sure to leave some edge space for taping to the mug. When you are done taping the mustache template on the mug properly such that the paint will not drip within the paper while you paint it, start painting. When the paint dries out, you can now present the gift to your dad.

Craft 78: Daddy's Car Wash Kit

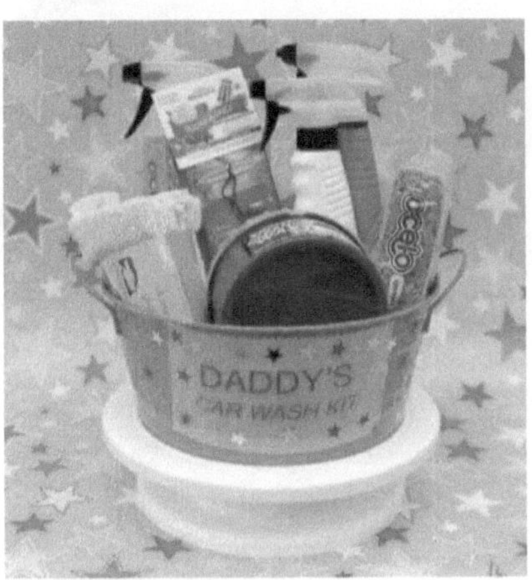

Materials

- Bucket
- Paint/ decorations
- Car washing products

Directions

1. Look for a bucket that is big enough to hold your dad's entire car washing products. Take some of the paint/decorations and decorate the bucket, you should have the words "Daddy's Car Wash Kit" standout. Make sure that the decorations and paint you use are waterproof so that they do not start fading in no time. Get the products that you dad likes to use on his car the most and put them in the bucket.

Craft 79: A Jumbo Tape Dispenser

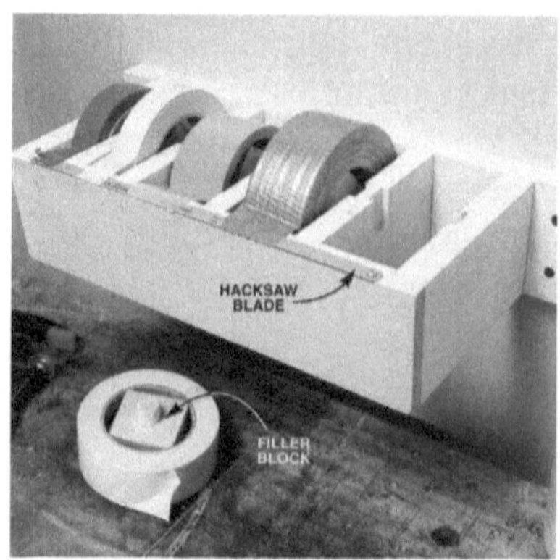

Materials

- Hacksaw blade
- Tapes
- Plywood
- Filler blocks
- Nails
- Saw
- Tape measure

Directions

1. First of all, this is not a gift to be made by a toddler, let you eleven or twelve years old try it. Take the plywood and use it to make a rectangular shelf like rack. Use the tape measure to make accurate spaces on the rack based on the wideness of the tapes that your daddy uses. Take the hacksaw blade and nail in one edge of the dispenser such that it can be used for cutting the tape when you are using it.

2. Cut the filler blocks into square blocks that can be able to cover the entire diameter in the middle of the tape. The average diameter is about three inches wide. The edges of the filler blocks should be a little bit rounded so that it fits properly. In each of the small compartments of the dispenser, make some holes where the filler block is going to be put. The edges of the filler block should be circular so that the tape can be easily used.

Craft 80: A Tie Rack

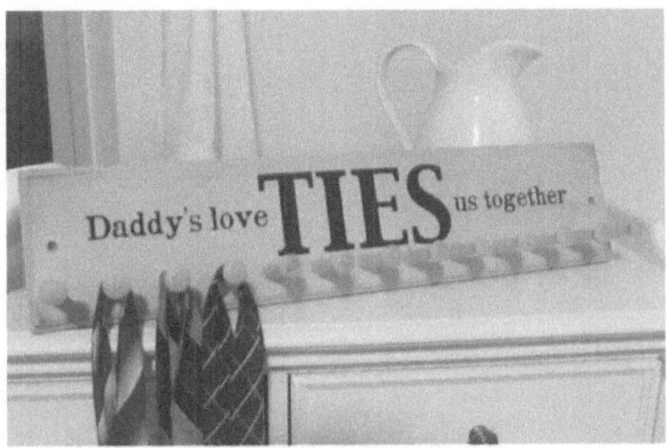

Materials

- Wood
- Saw
- Glue
- Drill
- Pencil
- Wooden dowel
- Decorations/paint

Directions

1. Take the rectangular wood and cut it down to around twenty inches or less based on the number of ties your daddy has. The piece of wood should also be four inches wide and with thickness of three inches. Take the piece of wood and sand it properly till all its edges are smooth. Use the pencil to mark holes on the piece of wood where the pegs will go. Make sure that they are about one and a half inches apart. You can even make some marks on the other side of the rack.

2. Take the drill and mark a half inch on its drilling bit to ensure that the holes are all half an inch deep. Then drill the wood on either one or both sides depending on the number of ties your dad owns. Take the wooden dowel and cut all the pegs that you will need from it. Make them three inches long so that they are able to hold your dad's ties comfortably. Take the glue and apply it to the pegs and insert them firmly to the holes you drilled on the rack. Now

take the decorations and decorate the rack, you can even fix some "Best Dad Ever" compliment quotations.

Craft 81: Monogrammed Cuff Links

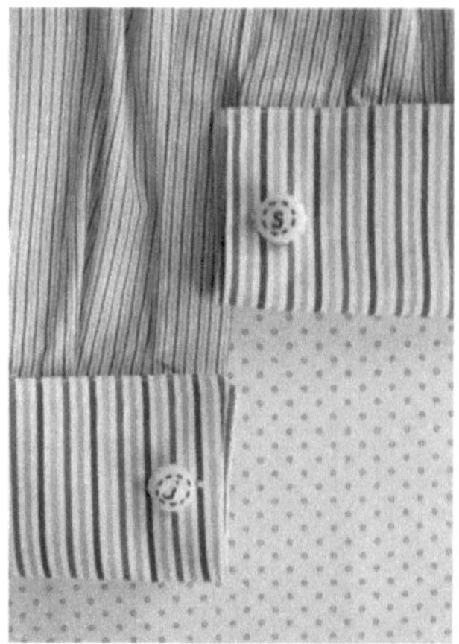

Materials

- White cloth
- Simple cufflink blanks
- Scissors
- Colored thread
- Sewing needle
- Pencils
- Cotton

Directions

1. Take the simple cufflink blanks and place them on the white cloth, take the pencil and use it to make the area around the cufflink blank. Make two of these and add some working space around the circles you have marked. Take the thread and the sewing needle and on the circles you made with the cufflink blank, sew the initials of your father's name. Take the scissors and cut out the two big circles with the initials or your dad's name. Thread your needle and stitch a hem that is one of a sixteenth of an inch, make it such that it folds on the wrong side.

2. Take a pinch of cotton the size of a button and place it on the hem of the white cloth, then place the cufflink blanks in place and just pull the thread to clinch the hem around the cufflinks stem. Then just tie a tight knot and use the scissors to cut the thread that remains hanging loose.

Craft 82: Best Dad Cards

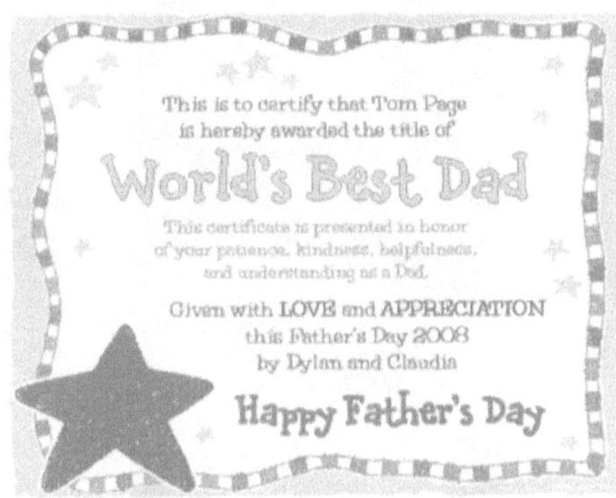

Materials

- Paper
- Scissors
- Pencil
- Colors
- Images
- Glue

Directions

1. To make a card for your dad for Father's Day, you will first need to think and come up with an interesting and personal theme. Make it a message a gratitude for the good that you dad has been doing for both you and your family. Take the paper that you will be using for the card, and use the scissors to cut it in to shape. If you are looking to write a long message and maybe even add some memorable images of your family, cut a big card and fold it several times.

2. Use the pencil to draw and write the message that you want to give your father. If you have any images that you would want him to have of you and him, attach them with the glue. Take the colors and decorate the card according to the theme that you are using. Fold it and then hand it to your daddy on Father's Day.

Craft 83: Generation Photograph

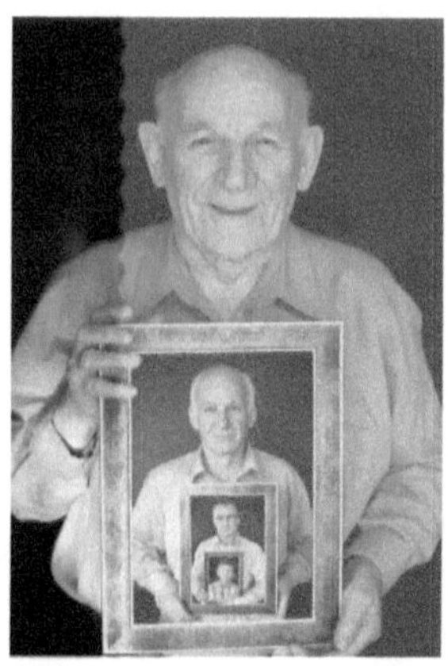

Materials

- A big frame
- Photographs of different sizes
- Glue
- Scissors

Directions

1. When you are making a generation photograph you will need pictures of your great grandfather, your grandfather, your father and yourself. The picture of your great grandfather should be the biggest followed by your grandfather's, your father's and then yours. Place them starting with the biggest followed by the bigger to the smallest. If there is a picture that is not in line, use the scissors to ensure that they fall in line.

2. Use the glue to stick them together once they have formed a nice picture like the one you are looking for. Wait till the glue dries up and the picture looks like one and then put it in the frame. Use a

gift wrapper to wrap it and hand it to your dad on Father's Day as a token of appreciation.

Craft 84: Father's Day Grill Apron

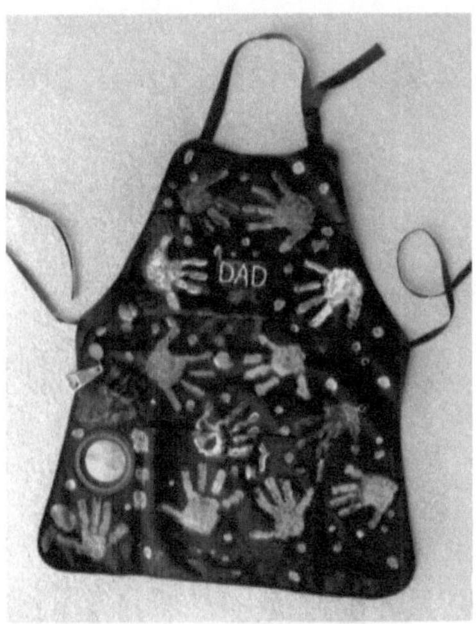

Materials

- Fabric paint
- Letter stencils
- Huge material
- Apron
- Pencil
- Scissors
- Double fold bias tape

Directions

1. Take the apron that you already own and place it on the huge cloth and use the pencil to mark where it reaches. When you lift up the apron, you will live an image of an apron on the cloth. Take the scissors and use them to cut out the apron from the big cloth. Use the double fold bias tape to cover the edges of the apron so that it looks neat.

2. Take the fabric paint and make your hand print and those of your siblings on the apron using some of dad's favorite colors. In case

you want to write a small message such as "Happy Father's Day", you can use the letter stencils. Use the remaining materials to make straps for the apron and attach them on their respective places, around the neck and the waist. With that you have completed the apron, now it is time to present it to your father.

Craft 85: A Tie with Your Handprint

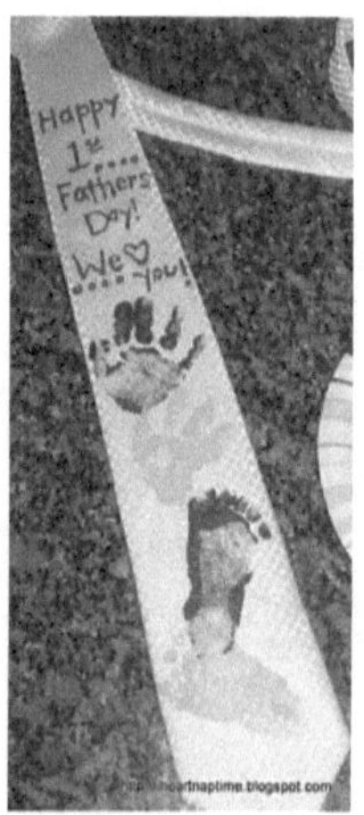

Materials

- A tie
- Fabric paint
- Letter stencil

Directions

1. This is easy but will be sentimental to your dad when he receives it. Take a tie that you have bought and use the fabric paint to make hand prints of yourself and your siblings. If you have a very young sibling, you can even include a footprint. Use the letter stencils to let your dad know that he is the best and wish him a happy Father's Day.

Craft 86: Father's Day Wreath

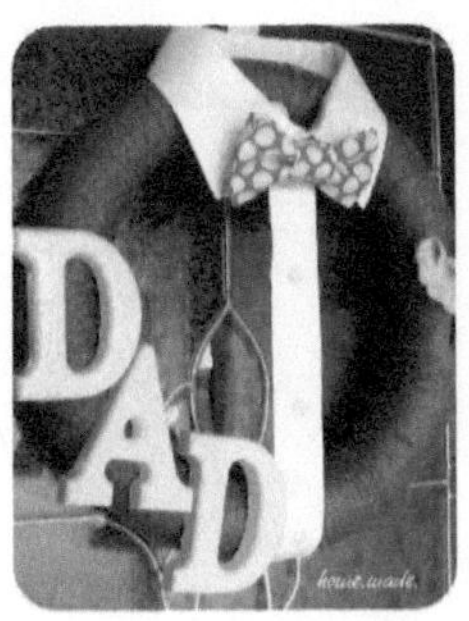

Materials

- Scissors
- Glue
- Tie
- Decorations (buttons)
- Block "DAD" letters
- A premade wreath

Directions

1. Take a colorful tie and place it across the wreath to measure the length. Cut off the extra part of the tie using the scissors. Use the glue to attach the tie to wreath, hold it down firmly till it sticks properly. The tie should be stuck with a design in mind.

2. Take the three block DAD letters and stick them on the wreath using the glue. Place them strategically in a way that complements the tie. Take your other decorations such as buttons or small flowers and glue them on the wreath and on the name to make it look beautiful. After the whole handmade wreath dries and the decorations are all in place, present it your dad.

Craft 87: Dad Rocks Paperweight

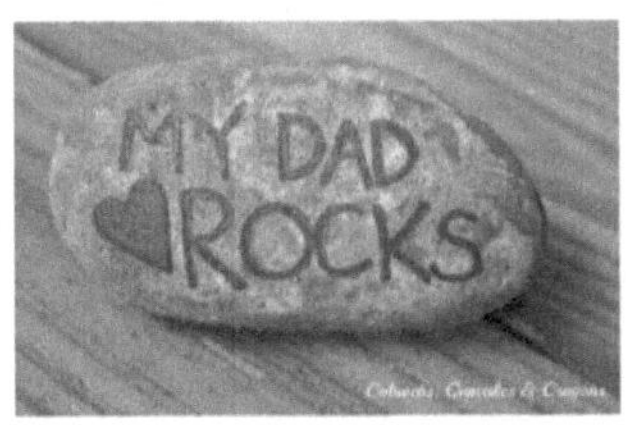

Materials

- Glitter glue
- A rock
- Paint (your dad's favorite)
- Paintbrush
- Water and soap
- Towel
- Acrylic sealer

Directions

1. The rock that you decide to use should be heavy enough to with stand the force of wind and hold the papers in place. Wash the stone with water and soap till it is thoroughly clean, dry it using the towel. Leave it in the open for some time to dry completely.

2. Take your dads favorite color and use the paintbrush to paint the whole rock. Leave it to dry and then apply a second lay of the same paint. You can now apply the glitter glue on the rock and let it to dry before writing the words "Dad Rocks". Leave the stone to dry completely and then use a gift wrapper to make it presentable and give it to your dad.

Craft 88: Finger Print Mug

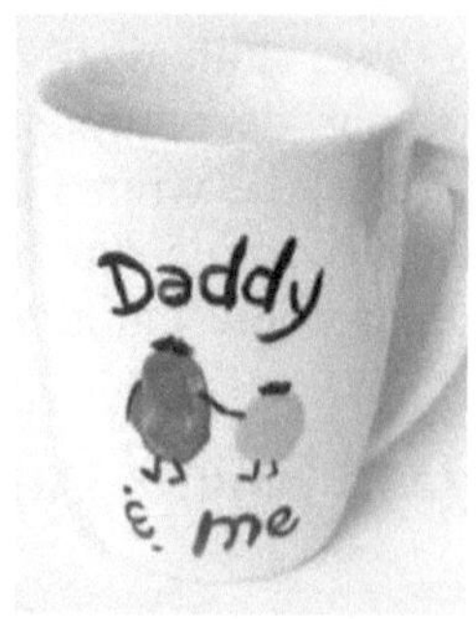

Materials

- A mug
- Permanent paint
- Oven

- Permanent marker

Directions

1. Take the mug and use the permanent paint to make two fingerprints on its side. Make a big finger print and a small one. Use the permanent marker to write a small personal message and to draw hands and feet on the two fingerprints. The fingerprints should look like two people holding hands, you and your dad.

2. Bake the mug in the oven at around three hundred and fifty degrees for half an hour and then allow it to cool. As you present the gift to your dad, let him know that it can only be hand washed to avoid the fading of the paint.

Craft 89: Monster Hand Card

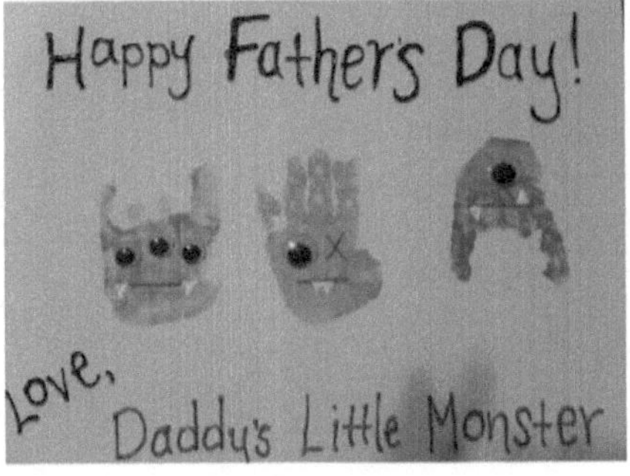

Materials

- A big piece of hard paper
- Several types of paint
- Shiny buttons
- Glue
- Permanent marker
- Paint

Directions

1. To make the card more personal use your hands and the paint to make hand prints in several different angles using different colors of paint. Turn the hand print into a head of a monster and make

sure that the print has a mouth and eyes. Use the shiny buttons as the eyes of the monster, glue them firmly on to the paper. Use the permanent marker to add a message that you would like to send to your father.

Craft 90: Best Daddy Ever Beans

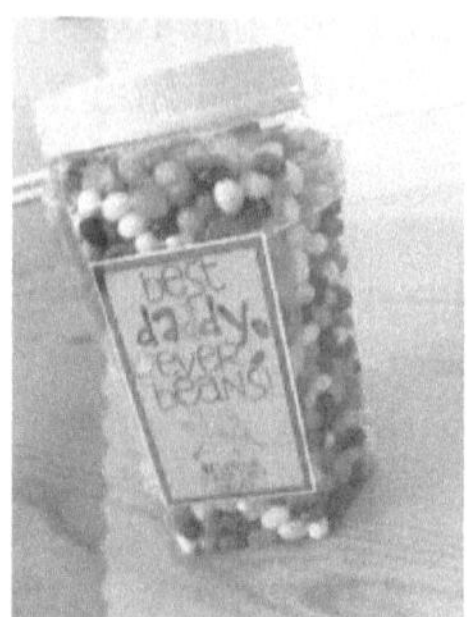

Materials

- Different colored beans
- A large bottle
- Paper
- Pen
- Marker
- Paper

Directions

1. Take a big clean bottle and fill it up with jelly beans of different colors. Take the paper and cut it into two equal parts the fit the bottle on the front and the back. On the paper that is on the front side, write a message wishing your dad a happy Father's Day using the marker.

2. The paper that goes on the back should have qualities that your father possesses based on the color of the jelly beans. Write down the qualities using the pen, they may include qualities such as devoted playful, respectful, forgiving and jovial. Use the glue to stick the two papers on their respective parts on the bottle and close it. Present it to your dad on Father's Day.

Craft 91: Shadow Photography

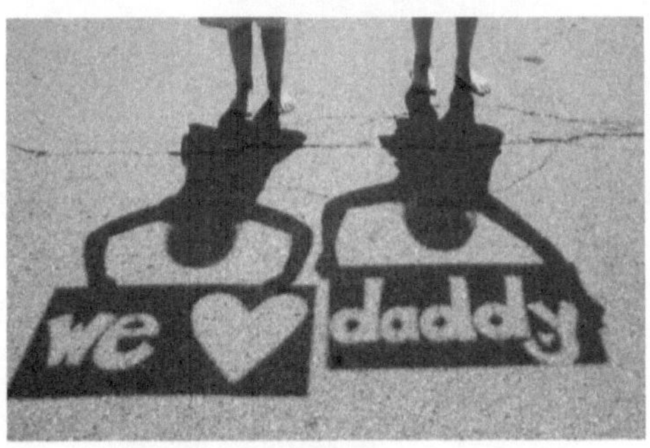

Materials

- Paper
- Scissors
- Camera
- Pencil
- Gift wrapper
- Frame

Directions

1. For this activity, you will need your siblings and your mum to help you out. Take the paper and use the pencil to write down a message such as "We Love Daddy" or any other that you want to send your dad.

2. Use the scissors to cut out the words from the big paper such that you are left with window like writings. Have your siblings hold the cards high up and strategically facing the sun such that the words are seen on the ground. Use the camera to take a photo of the shadow and print the photo. You can now frame and finally wrap the photo and present it to your daddy on Father's Day.

Craft 92: I Love You This Much Card

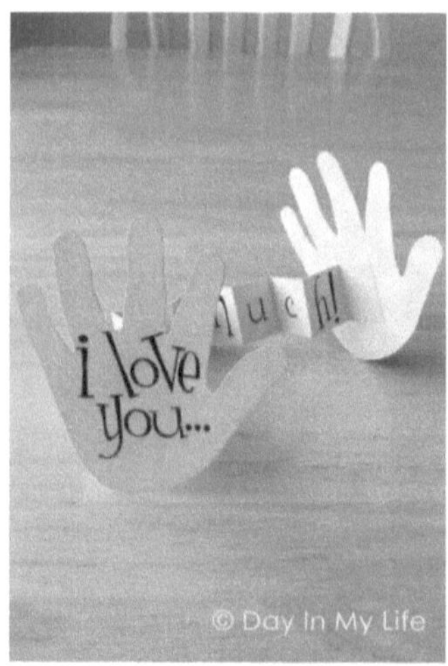

Materials

- Paper
- Marker
- Scissors
- Glue
- Pencil
- Paint

Directions

1. Take a hard chart paper and use a pencil to draw around your handprints. Use the scissors to cut around such that you are left with the handprints alone. Paint them your dads favorite color on the front side of each alone, leave the inner side as it was.

2. Write some the words "I Love You" on the front sides of both the palms. Cut a long rectangular paper and write the words "This Much!" Attach both the palms with the long rectangular paper. Such that when you stretch it out it is super long. Folder the paper used to hold both the palms such that only the palms are visible. Present it to your dad on Father's Day and have him stretch it out.

Craft 93: Couch Potato Gift Basket

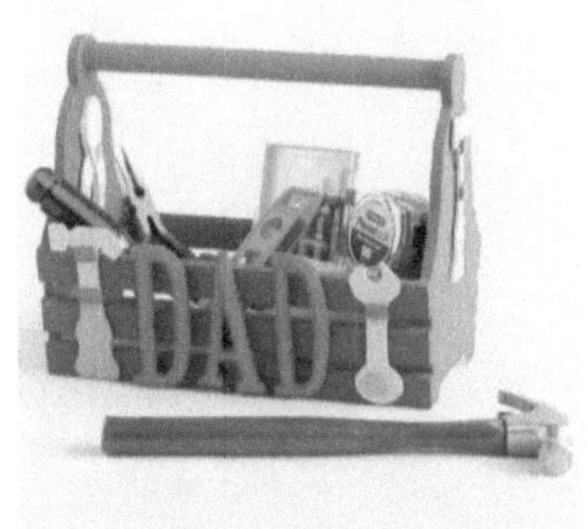

Materials

- Remote
- His favorite snacks
- Movies
- A basket
- Marker
- Paper
- Decorations

Directions

1. You will take the marker and use it to write a message to your dad on the paper. Then use the decorations to make the basket look nice and presentable. Take all the items mentioned above and put them in the basket. Present it to your dad and just let him have a relaxing day. Also make sure that you take care of anything that he is supposed to be doing at home so that he is not distracted.

Craft 94: Bow Tie Card

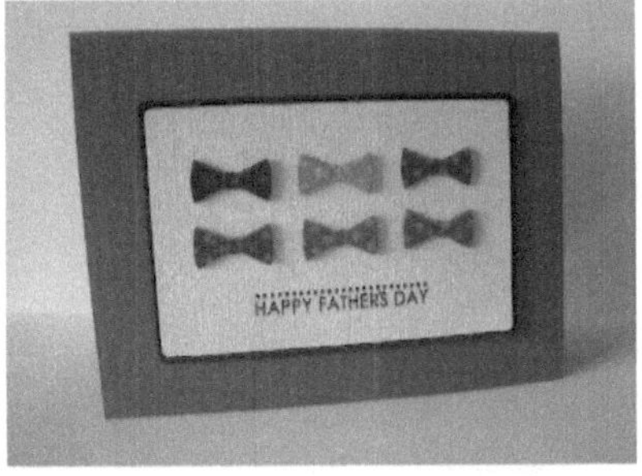

Materials

- Several hard papers
- Scissors
- Glue
- Pencil
- Colors
- Pens

Directions

1. Take a big paper and draw some bow ties on it using the pencil. Color them differently to have some variety. Use the scissors to cut out the bow ties, make sure that you make about six nice bow ties. Use the glue to stick them on another paper which you should first color to complement the bow ties. Use the pens to write a Happy Father's Day message for your dad. Now you can present it for it is complete.

Craft 95: Candy Gram Poster

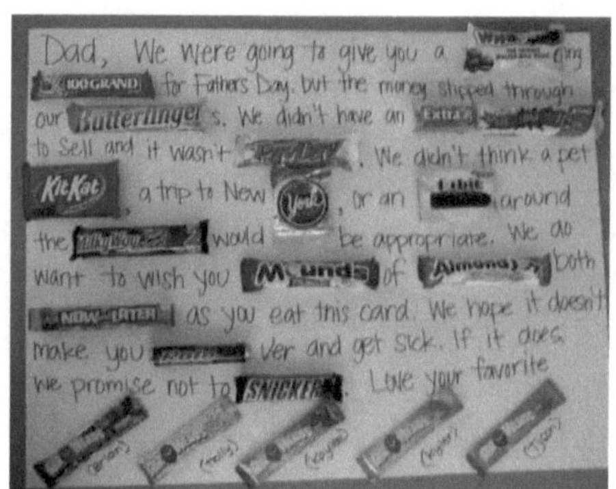

Materials

- Different brands of candy
- Paper
- Glue
- Marker
- Pencil

Directions

1. Take a big paper and use a pencil to mark spaces that will be left blank for the candy. Take the marker and write down the message skipping the spaces that will be filled by the candy bars. Take all the candy and use the glue to stick them on their rightful places. After the glue is dry, it is ready for you to present it to your father.

Craft 96: Soda Bottle Covers

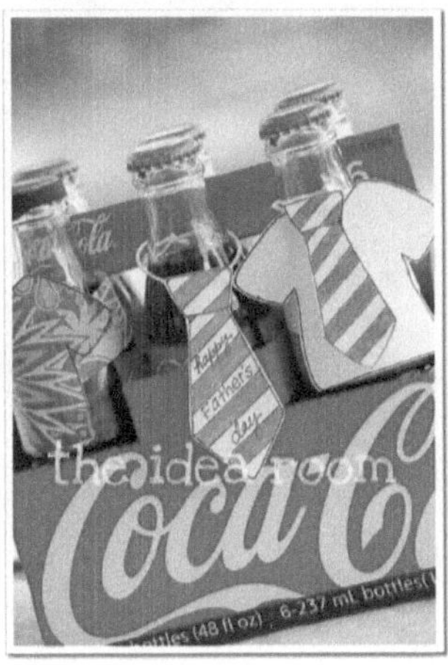

Materials

- Paper
- Scissors
- Glue
- Pencil
- Colors
- Pens

Directions

1. Take the paper and use the pencil to draw ties and shirts with ties on them. Use the color to make the ties and shirts interesting and colorful. Use the pens of different colors to write an interesting Father's Day message. Use the scissors to cut out the complete ties and the shirts with ties. Cut a strip of paper and attach it using the

glue to make a noose on the tie, it will go around the top of the bottle.

Craft 97: Father's Day Trophy

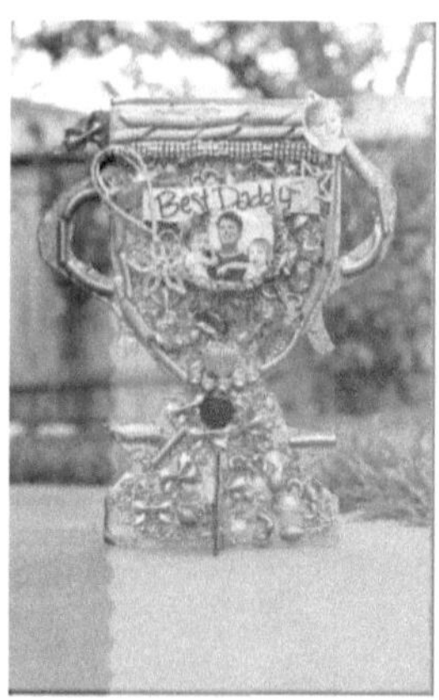

Materials

- One big paper cup
- A square box
- Masking tape
- Gold or silver paint
- Scissors
- Paint brush
- Black construction paper
- Glue
- Paper

Directions

1. Take your masking tape and use it to cover the whole of the square box. Then take the paper cup and attach it to the box using the glue. Use the scissors to cut out handles from the paper and use the glue to stick them to both sides of the paper cup. Take the masking tape and use it to cover all over the paper cup and the square box.

2. From there, take the gold or silver paint and use the paint brush to paint the whole of the trophy. Take the black construction paper and write the words "World's Best Dad" using the white pen. Then

stick it on the front side of the square box. You now have a trophy for your dad.

Craft 98: Golf Course Pen Holder

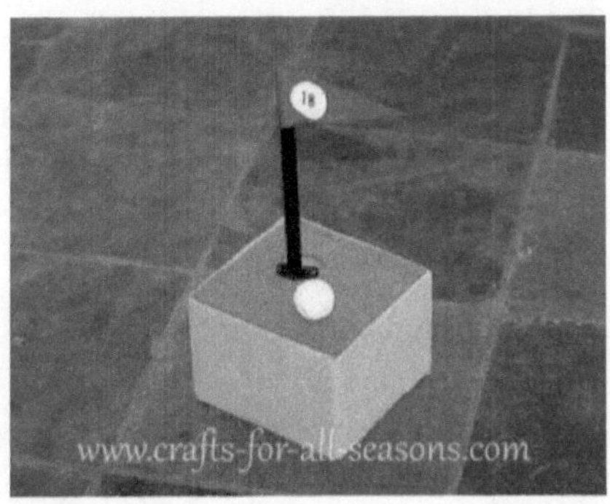

Materials

- Pens
- Block of silk flower foam oasis
- Dark green square felt (same size as the top of the silk block)
- Scissors
- Glue
- Large light green felt (enough to cover the whole silk block)
- Small spoon
- Coffee beans
- Clothespin
- White marble
- A coin
- Exacto knife
- Colored card

Directions

1. Place the coin on the foam oasis and trace around it with a pen. Take the exacto knife and cut alongside the lines you made with your pen. Use the small spoon to scoop out the foam oasis you are cutting out. Place the dark green square felt on the foam oasis and trace the circle, cut it out so that your felt has a hole on the same place as the foam oasis.

2. Take the glue and spread it on the dark green felt and then attach it to the foam oasis. Take the scissors and cut accurate light green felt into shape and use the glue to stick it around the foam oasis. Take the colored card (your dad's favorite color) and cut it in to a flag shape of your choosing. You can have a message on the flag telling your dad that he is the best. The pen will be the flag pole for your flag. Use the marble as the golf ball and place it next to the hole on the foam oasis. Put some coffee beans in the hole so that the pen does not fall when you place it in. Now you have completed the golf course pen holder and you can present it to your dad.

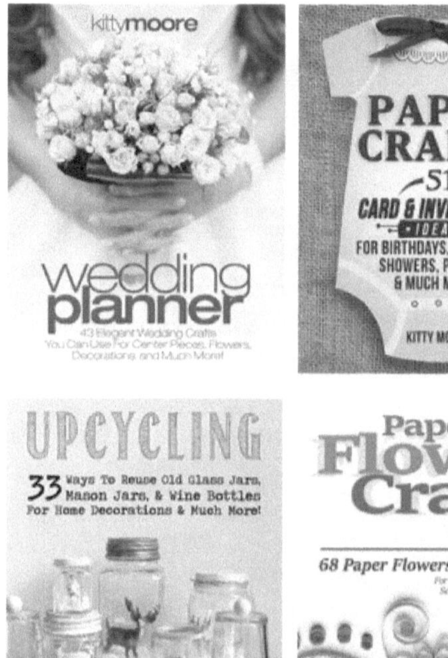

Check out Kitty's books at:

ArtsCraftsAndMore.com/go/books

Craft 99: Luggage Handle Cover

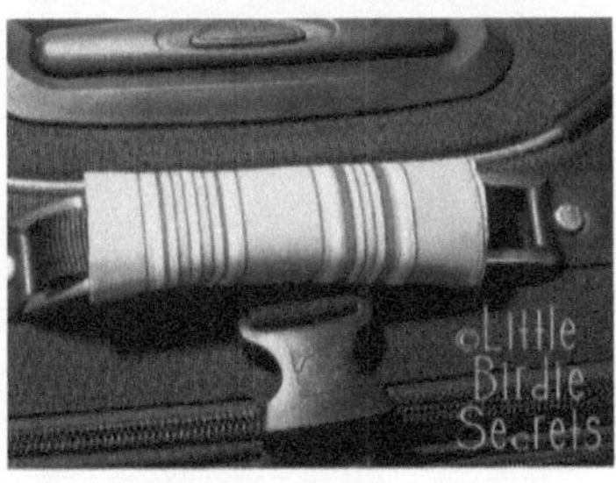

Materials

- Piece of cloth
- Thread
- Scissors
- Needle
- Pencil
- Rule

Directions

1. Use the ruler to get the exact measurements that you will require for the handle cover and use the pencil to mark them on the cloth. Take the scissors and cut along the marks such that you are left with the piece of cloth that you will be using only. Fold the cloth into the desirable shape and after threading your needle, start sewing the cloth. Sew it close around the handle of your dads travelling bag. This is an awesome gift to a dad who travels a lot for work.

Craft 100: Pocket Watch Accordion Photo Album

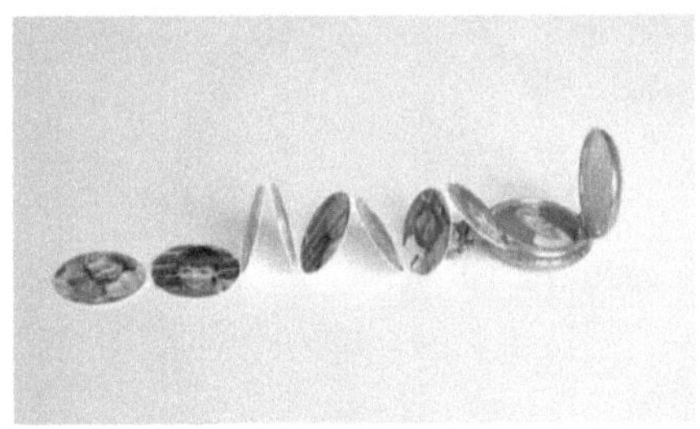

Materials

- Pocket watch
- Small photos of the family (passport photo size).
- Scissors
- Glue
- Pencil
- Compass

Directions

1. Take compass and pencil and use them to draw accurate circles that are equal to the size of the pocket watch. Cut out the parts that are out of the circle and leave small sleeves on either side of the circle. Use the glue to attach the circular photos using the small sleeves on the sides of the circles. The primary photo will be glued on the inside of the pocket watch. All you have to do now is to wait for the glue to dry and then fold he photos and place them inside the pocket watch.

Craft 101: Soda Can Coasters

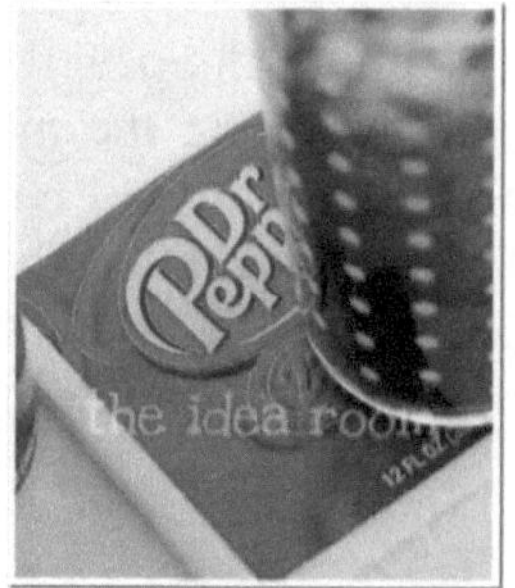

Materials

- Empty soda cans
- Scissors
- Glue
- White square ceramic tiles
- Paint brush
- Small squeegee

Directions

1. Take the scissors and cut of both the top and the bottom part of the soda can. Then cut the remaining part of the tin such that you are left a rectangular shape sheet of tin. Cut the tin sheet into a square of about four inches by four inches. Use the brush and spread the glue on the inner side of the tin and then attach it to the white ceramic tile. Use the small squeegee to spread out the glue between the surface of the tin and the tile.

2. Look for some heavy objects and place them on the complete coaster so that the glue sticks firmly. Scrap off the glue appearing on the sides and your coasters are done. Make several so that your daddy has enough for his man cave and office.

Craft 102: Family Handprint Gift

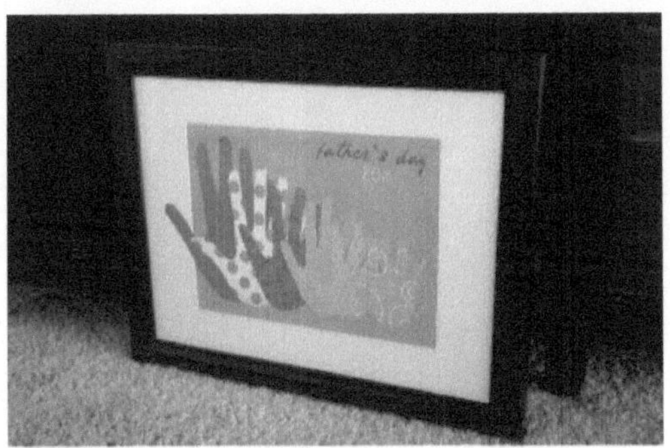

Materials

- Paint (different colors)
- A4 size piece of paper
- Frame
- Scissors

Directions

1. Take the paper and use the scissors to cut it into shape such that it fits in the frame. Take the different colors that your dad is fond of and have the whole family make their handprints on the paper. Use the marker to write a message of appreciation from the whole

family to your dad. Place the decorated paper in the frame and present it to your father on Father's Day.

Craft 103: Why We Love You

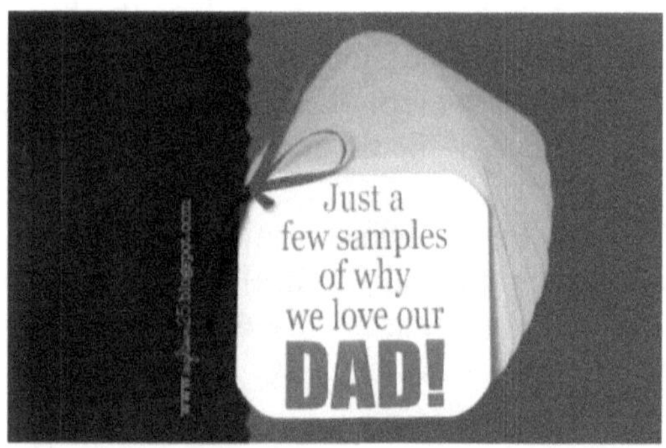

Materials

- Pen
- Marker
- Small plain cards
- Ribbon
- Scissors
- Paper punch

Directions

1. Take the cards and use the scissors to cut them into the shape that you want your small booklet to have. Use your paper puncher to make holes on the edge of all your cards so that you will have an easy time binding them.

2. Take both the pen and marker and write reasons why you love your dad on the cards. Use pens and markers of different colors to make it interesting. Finally use the ribbon to bind the complete cards together to form a small book. Now all you have to do is to wait for the big day and present your father with the gift.

Craft 104: Spooky Cauldron Punch

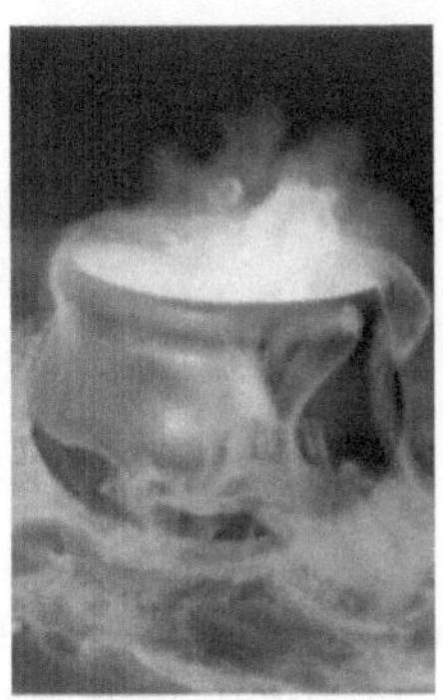

Materials

- Dry ice
- 1 large punch bowl
- 1 smaller punch bowl that will fit into the large one

Directions

1. Make your punch as normal and place the punch bowl into the larger bowl. Using tongs, put pieces of dry ice into the space in between the two bowls – it is important that you do not touch it as it will burn. Just before you are ready to serve, carefully pour some hot water into the outer bowl. This will cause the dry ice to start smoking.

Craft 105: Spooky Mirror

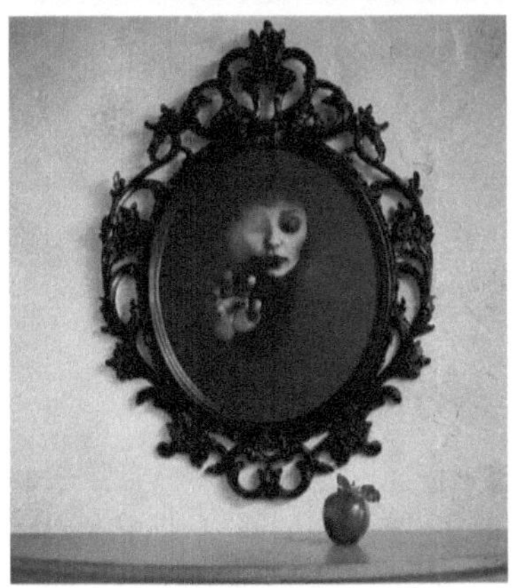

Materials

- A frame painted black or silver
- Reflective paint
- A ghostly picture and a mirror image of the same shot

Directions

1. Take out the glass and lay it face up on the table. Tape the mirror image to the glass and then turn the glass over. Spray on the reflective paint at the back, taking care not to cover the face and hands. Set aside to dry. Remove the picture and put the glass back in the frame, with the painted side to the back. Glue the original picture to the backing and put the frame back together again.

Craft 106: Awesome Halloween Lighting

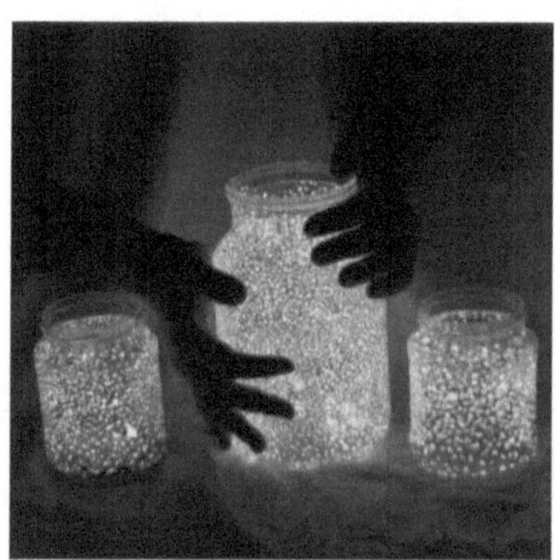

Materials

- 2 mason jars, thoroughly cleaned
- Paint that glows in the dark in different colors
- A fine paintbrush
- Plain water

Directions

1. Shake or stir the paint until it is completely combined. Using your first color, stipple the paint onto the inside of the jar. Allow it to dry for a bit. Then carry on with the next color. You can have as

many or as few colors as you like. Then set it in the sun so that it can soak up all the sunlight and be prepared to be wowed at night.

Craft 107: Eerie Severed Head

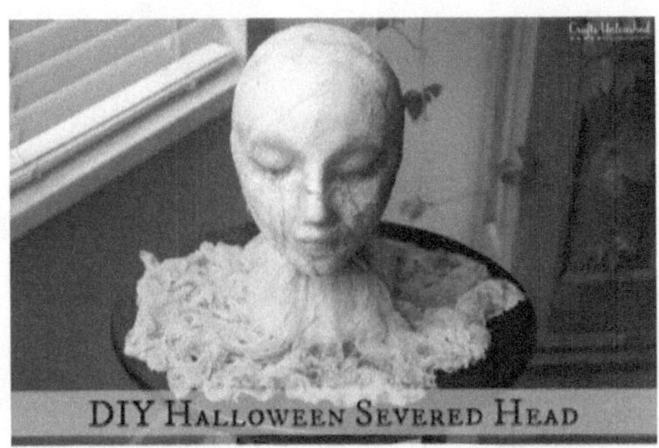

Materials

- A fabric stiffener or strong cornstarch solution
- A display head made from foam
- Loose weave cheese cloth
- Mod Podge that dries hard
- A foam brush
- An ink pad and black ink
- Natural twine
- Coffee
- A baking tray

Directions

1. Start off by dying the cloth. Plain coffee – no milk, no sugar, is all you need. You do need a strong coffee though. Don't stress too much if not all the coffee dissolves as this can leave a nice speckled effect. Submerge the cloth and swish it around a bit. Remove and wring out and hang up to dry. While it is drying, start applying black ink onto the head, around about where shadows would naturally appear so that it looks more realistic. If you like, you can also start sponging other ink colors onto the head. Set aside to dry.

2. When the cloth is dry, scrunch it up and put it into a bowl and add the paste of corn starch or stiffener. Work it into the fabric so that

it is completely covered. You want it to be able to hold a spherical shape. Smooth out the cloth and drape over the craft head, putting everything on the baking tray. Make sure that it drapes properly and the cloth drapes nicely around the "body". Set aside to dry. Once dry, use a sponge to coat the cheese cloth in Mod Podge so that it sticks to the head. Leave to dry. You can trim the bottom of the cheese cloth to make it look better and use the scraps to make your head look even creepier.

Craft 108: Alternative to Pumpkins

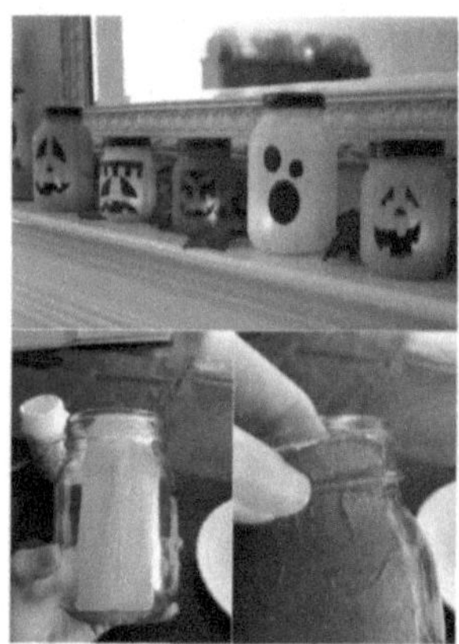

Materials

- Jars with smooth sides and no writing
- Black acrylic paint
- Adhesive tape
- Different colors of tissue paper
- Scissors
- A paint brush
- Modge Podge
- Some black construction paper
- Electric tea light candles

Directions

1. Take the lids off all the jars and, if using mason jars, use the adhesive to keep the removable portion in place. Paint the outside of the lid black and set aside to dry. Cut the tissue paper into strips

to a size so that it will fit snugly on the outside of the jar. Center the jar on the sheets of tissue paper and lightly trace the bottom. Apply Modge Podge to the bottom of the jar and adhere the circle section that you drew. Apply a layer of Modge Podge just big enough for the strip you are working with and apply the paper a little at a time smoothing as you go along. Repeat until the whole outside of the jar, barring the rim where the lid screws on, is covered. Continue in the manner, each strip overlapping the last until your jar is done. Set aside to dry.

2. In the interim, make the faces – cut out eyes, noses, etc. from the black paper and glue to the bottle with Modge Podge when the tissue paper has dried. Alternatively, you can draw on the faces yourself using markers. Put the tea light into the jar, and close the lid, ready to use.

Craft 109: Make Your Own Ghost

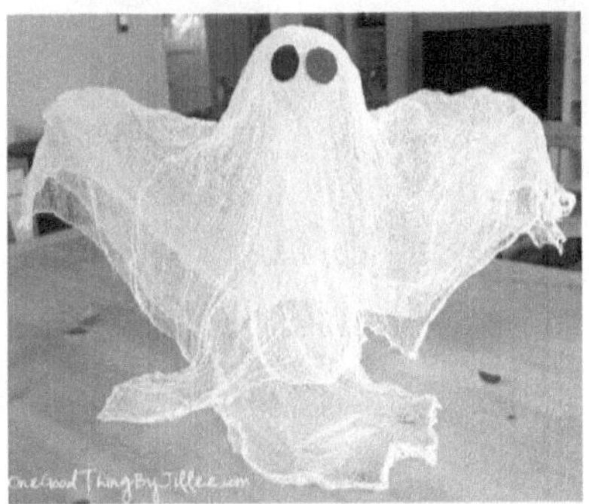

Materials

- A large, soda bottle and adhesive tape
- Corn starch or fabric starch
- A square of cheese cloth
- A ball
- Heavy gauge wire

Directions

1. Assemble your ghost form – place the ball on top of the soda bottle and tape in place. Make your arms out of the wire and tape into place. Throw the cheese cloth over to see the basic effect. Adjust

the form as necessary. Soak the cheese cloth in a strong solution of starch. Wring out and arrange over the form. You need to ensure that there is a good deal of "ghost" touching the ground to make the model more stable. Set aside to dry completely.

2. Once dry, remove the soda bottle, wire and ball. Attach a set of googly eyes or draw on your own eyes with a permanent marker. If you have done it right, this should stand on its own two "feet". If it won't stand, you can always string it up with fishing wire for a good effect.

Craft 110: Bewitched Cookies

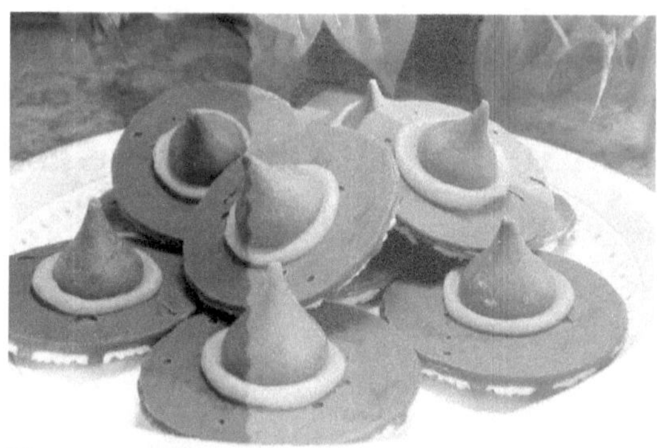

Materials

- Hershey's kisses (unwrapped)
- Chocolate dipped biscuits
- Frosting in orange

Directions

1. Place the biscuits, chocolate side up, on a plate and put a layer of orange frosting on them. Place a Hershey's Kiss in the center and squish it down a bit so that the frosting spreads. All done!

Craft 111: Halloween Favors

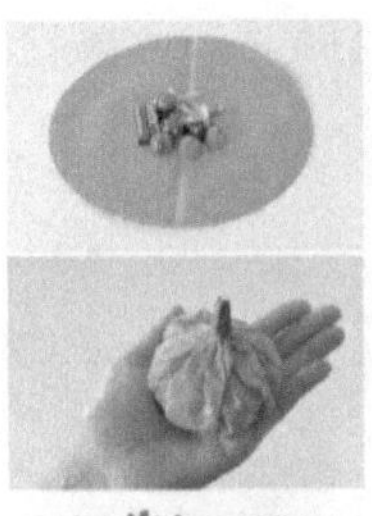
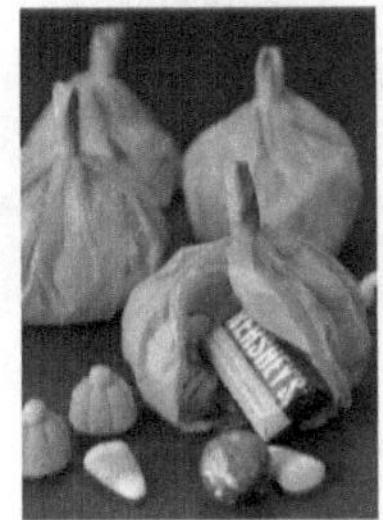

Materials

- Tissue or crepe paper in orange
- Floral tape in green
- Candy to go inside
- A 9-inch circle template
- Scissors
- A pencil

Directions

1. Put down two pieces of tissue paper and trace around your circle template with a pencil. Cut the circles out. It is one sheet per pumpkin. Put the candy into the center – the more candy, the fatter your pumpkin. Take the little package into the palm of your hand and bunch it up. Twist the end closed so that you have a rough pumpkin shape. Secure the top with the floral tape.

Craft 112: The Eye of The Spider Vase

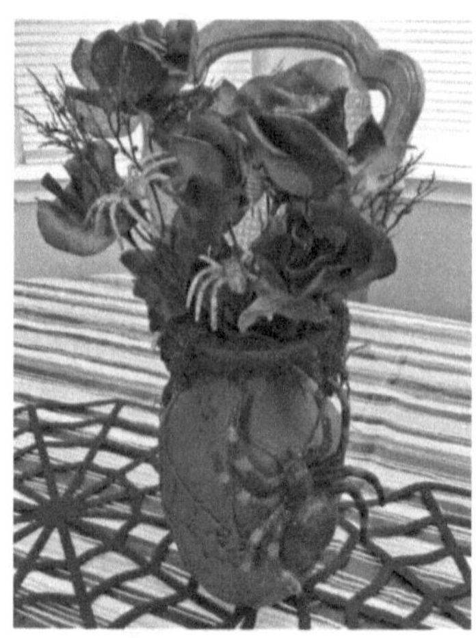

Materials

- A cheap or old, chipped vase
- Black paint with a matt finish
- Modge Podge
- Black lace
- Halloween inspired flowers and foliage
- A creepy spider decoration
- A hot glue gun
- A sponge brush

Directions

1. Paint the vase with a coat of Modge Podge and set aside to dry. Once the Modge podge has dried, draw on a spider's web using your hot glue gun. It can help to find a template online and place that inside the glass as a guide. Once the glue is dry, paint the whole vase, including the interior lip as far as you can see, black. Allow to dry and put a second coat on if necessary.

2. In the interim, if you like, you can decorate your creepy spider so that he has colors that match your flowers. Glue the spider to the vase with hot glue and let it set. Arrange the flowers and Halloween foliage in the vase to your liking and then drape the lace around the edge of the vase.

Craft 113: Shimmering Pumpkin

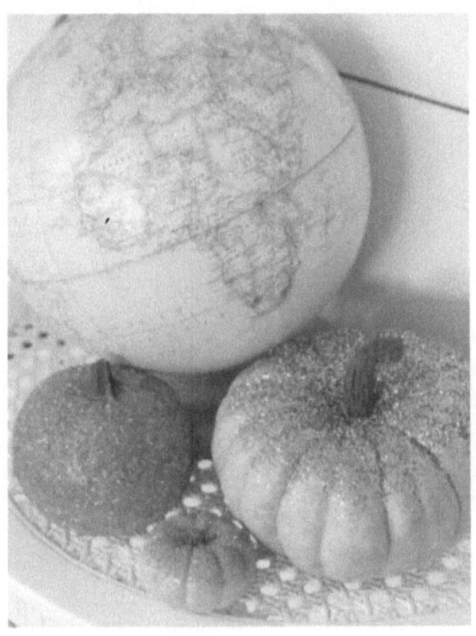

Materials

- Different sized pumpkins
- Colorful glitter
- A tablespoon
- A spray adhesive
- A fine paintbrush (optional)
- Craft paint in brown (optional)
- Scrap paper

Directions

1. Cover the pumpkin stem with painter's tape and spray a coat of adhesive over the rest of the area you want glittered. It is better to work in sections. Sprinkle glitter while the adhesive is still wet. Allow to dry and then shake off any glitter than didn't onto the paper. Funnel it back into your glitter bottle. If you want to apply glitter all over, repeat this process, this time tipping the pumpkin on it sides so that you can glitter the sides. Glittering the very base of the pumpkin is a waste of time and can create more mess.

Craft 114: A Different Take on The Pumpkin

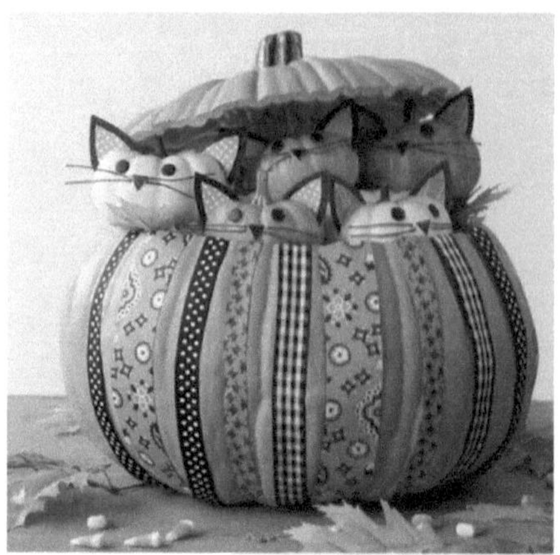

Materials

- Scissors
- Different lots of ribbon
- A big pumpkin with its guts taken out
- White glue
- Thumbtacks
- A template for a cat's ear and nose
- Cardstock in black
- A pencil
- Pretty scrapbook paper
- 5 little faux pumpkins
- A hot glue gun
- 10 thumb tacks or buttons or 5 pairs of googly eyes
- Black florist's wire
- 5 sharp pencils or thick skewers
- Oasis

Directions

1. You will start by decorating the big pumpkin. This is easily accomplished by gluing ribbon onto the base of the pumpkin and then gluing down all along one of the ribs and then securing on the inside of the pumpkin with the tacks. Cut 5 sets of ears out of the black card. Cut another five sets out of the scrapbooking paper,

ensuring that these are not as big as the black cards. Cut out 5 noses from the black card. Glue the patterned inner ears to the black card ears you made. Hot glue one set to each little pumpkin and then add on the nose.

2. Use craft glue to attach a patterned-paper inner ear to each black-card-stock outer ear. Let dry. Hot glue one pair of ears to each small pumpkin. You can then hot glue on whatever you have decided to use for the eyes. Cut twenty pieces of craft wire, an inch and a half in length to make your cats whiskers. Hot glue four whiskers to each cat. Put the oasis in the bottom of the big pumpkin and spike the faux pumpkins with the sharpened pencils or skewers. Place the other end in the oasis and arrange the kittens as you like. Put the lid of the pumpkin back on so that the kittens seem to be peeking out.

Craft 115: Spidery Webs

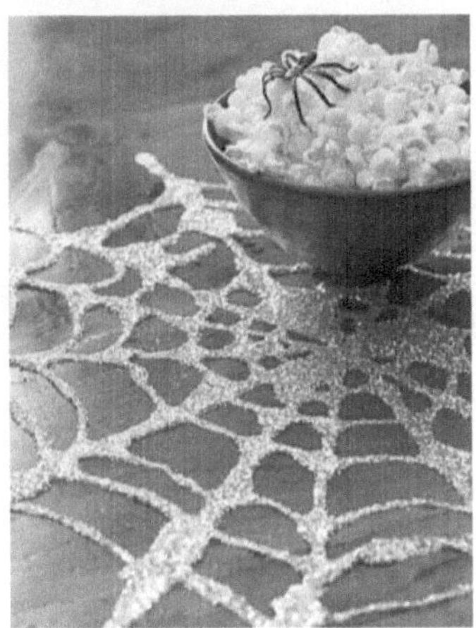

Materials

- Wax paper
- Elmer's glue (chilled for a couple of hours)
- Glitter
- A spider web template if necessary
- Adhesive tape

Directions

1. If you are using the template, place on the table and tape two sheets of wax paper onto it. Start drawing your spider web in the center, working your way out to the outer levels. Work fairly quickly. Sprinkle on copious amounts of glitter and set aside where it will be undisturbed for a couple of days. Once completely cured, tap to get rid of excess glitter and carefully remove from the paper.

Craft 116: Carve Pumpkins the Easy Way

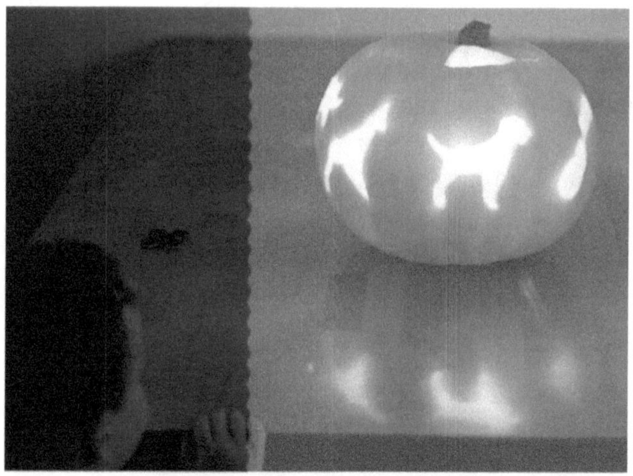

Materials

- A pumpkin of your choice, all the insides scooped out and clean
- Metal cookie cutters
- A rubber mallet
- A sharp knife to carve the pumpkin with

Directions

1. Determine where you want your cutouts on your pumpkin and then place the cookie cutter in the right spot. Working on one shape at a time, tap the cutter gently with your mallet so that the cookie cutter goes all the way through. If necessary, place the knife through to cut through tough bits and clean up as necessary.

Craft 117: Gorgeous Halloween Wreath

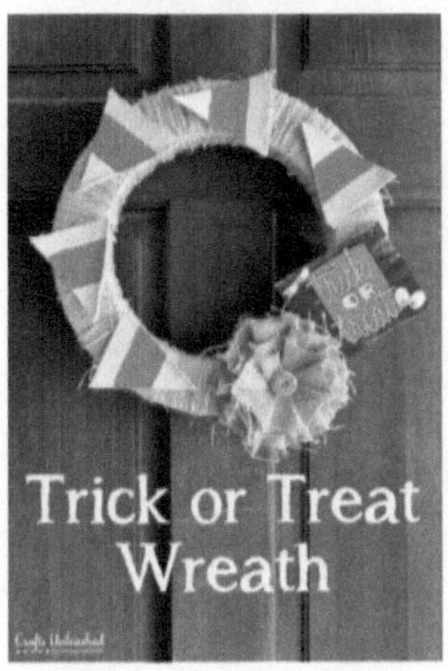

Materials

- A wreath base
- Raffia
- Craft paint in candy corn colors
- Bits of canvas offcuts
- Flowers made from burlap
- A hot glue gun
- Buttons
- Embellishments of your choice

Directions

1. Cover the base completely with raffia, securing using your hot glue gun. Cut the canvas pieces into triangles and paint a coat of white on them. Allow to dry before applying a strip of orange and then one of yellow so that it looks like candy corn. When dry, glue onto base. Make a focal point with the burlap flowers and buttons and whatever other embellishments you want to use and hot glue in place.

Craft 118: A Wreath That Is Good Enough to Eat

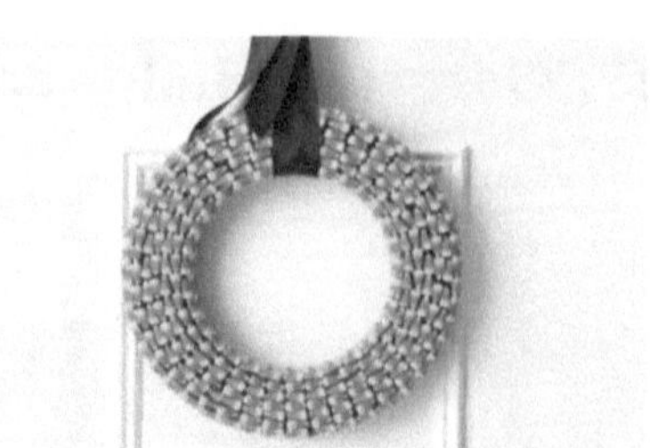

Materials

- Satin ribbon in black or chocolate brown
- Candy corns
- A wreath base
- A hot glue gun

Directions

1. Wrap the entire wreath base with the ribbon so that there are no gaps showing through. Glue in place with the hot glue gun. Then glue each little candy corn neatly in place so that they all line up – cover the front and sides of the wreath base. When done, thread some more ribbon through the center and tie a big bow on top so that you have something to hang the wreath with.

Craft 119: Illuminating Luminaries

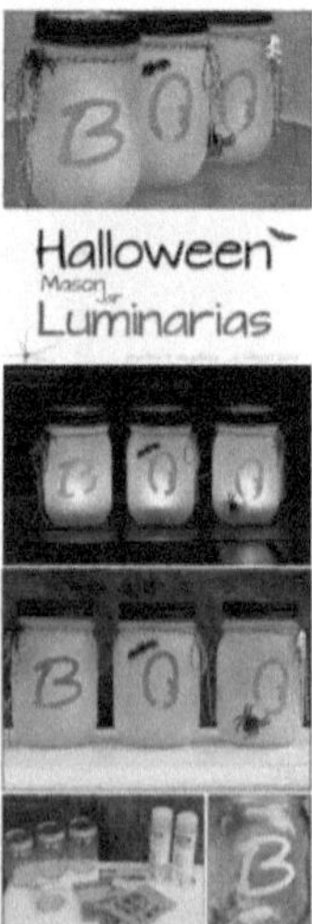

Materials

- Electric tea lights
- Glittery spray paint
- A sponge brush
- Frosted glass effect spray paint
- Embellishments of your choosing
- Decorated mason jar inserts for the lids
- Alphabet vinyl stickers
- Black acrylic paint
- Mason jars
- Natural twine

Directions

1. Stick the letters to the mason jars and apply the frost effect paint over the whole jar. Set aside to dry. Spray on a layer of the glittery paint and leave to dry. In the interim, spray paint the rings of the jars in black and set aside to dry. Once the paint on the bottles is dry, peel off the stickers and add whatever embellishments you like. When done, put the tea lights into the jar and close the bottle.

Craft 120: Pet Ghost

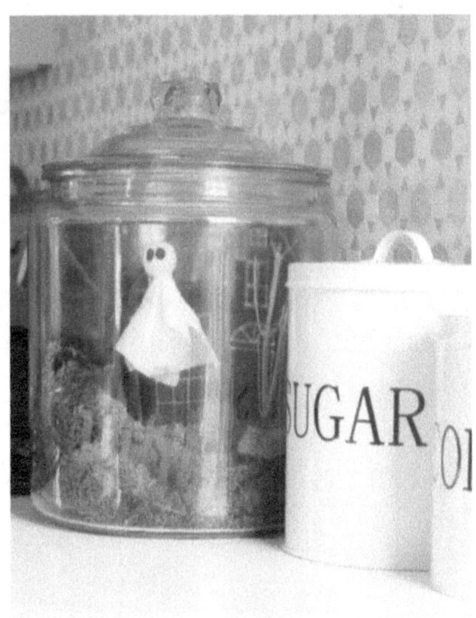

Materials

- A big clear jar
- Some sheet moss
- Some reindeer moss
- A few twigs out the garden
- Basic MDF house cutouts out (painted black)
- Chalk marker
- Scissors
- Clear fishing line
- Tissues (plain white0
- A ping pong ball
- A hot glue gun
- A fence cutout (painted)
- Wire snips
- Embellishments you want to add
- Double sided tape

Directions

1. On the base of the bell jar, layer your mosses to fit exactly and map the positions for your houses, etc. Draw on the windows and doors of your house with the chalk marker and place inside the jar. When you are happy with the position, tape in place using the double-sided tape. Put the twigs on your "lawn" to act as trees.

2. Tear one of the tissues roughly into equal halves and place one half on top of the other in the shape of a cross. Put the ball in the center and then scrunch the tissue round this to make a ghost. Secure with fishing line. Draw on the eyes or glue on googly eyes. Tie the fishing line tightly around the neck and attach the other end to the lid of the jar with clear tape. Add in the fence and any other finishing touches that you feel might be necessary and your terrarium is done.

Craft 121: Snow White's Apple

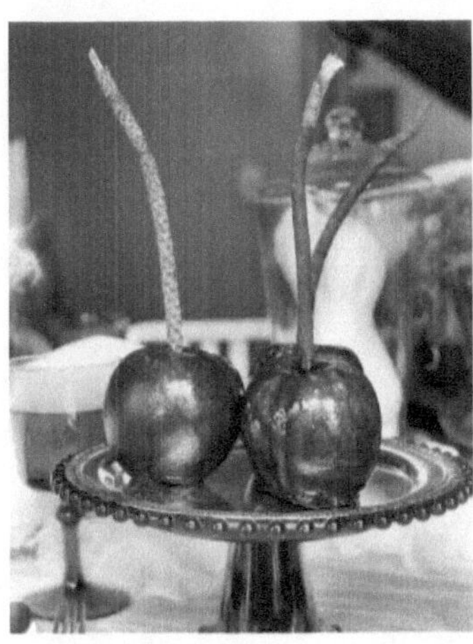

Materials

- Apples (any color, washed well)
- Dried twigs (cleaned up)
- Corn syrup (light)
- Baking sugar
- Cinnamon (infused oil)
- Water
- A candy thermometer
- Food coloring in black and red

Directions

1. Sharpen the end of the twig and spike the apple onto it. In a heavy-based pot, add the sugar, corn syrup and water and bring to the boil over a medium-low heat, stirring continuously. It is ready when all the sugar has dissolved and the temperature of the mixture is allowed to reach 300F.

2. Take it off the heat and add the remaining ingredients, not worrying to mix too well – a mottled look is good for the apples. Dip the apple in the mixture, ensuring that it is properly coated and set aside to cool on a sheet of non-stick baking paper.

Craft 122: Spooky Jars

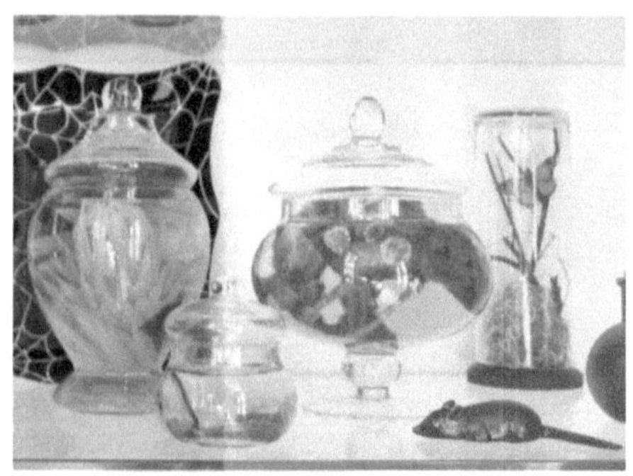

Materials

- A range of bell jars, clear cookie jars and specimen jars
- Food coloring in green
- Plastic animals or human body parts to use as specimens
- Water
- Different dried seeds or pods

Directions

1. Mix up the water with the food coloring so it is bright green. Add a drop or two of black to tone the color down and make it look dirtier if you like. Place your collection in the jars and practice your best mad scientist laugh. Cover all the "specimens" with your own brand of formaldehyde. Some should float, others should sink to the bottom of the jar to ensure variety and an extra aspect of creepiness.

Craft 123: Ghost Dance

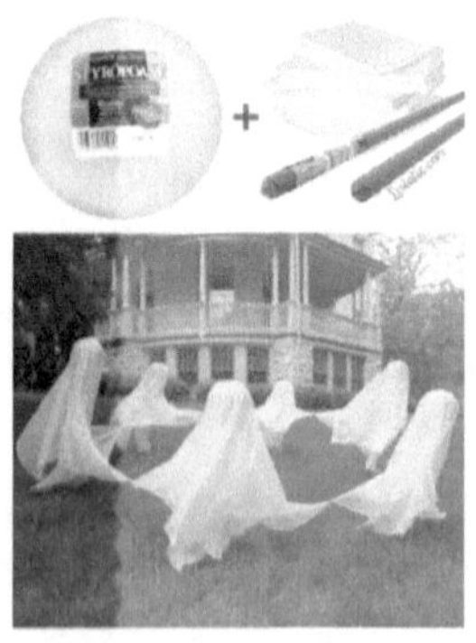

Materials

- 5 or 6 large Styrofoam balls about as big as your head (one for each ghost)
- Black paint
- 5 or 6 thick dowelling rods, as tall as you are for the bodies
- 5 or six sheets of pure white cotton, cheese cloth or muslin (does not have to be the most expensive type - thin cloth works best)

Directions

1. Paint the dowels black and set aside to dry. Once dry, stake them into the ground in a rough circular shape – one per ghost. Spike the Styrofoam heads onto the other end of the dowels, pushing them in up to about halfway. Drape the cloth sheets over the heads tying one corner of each to the corner of the sheet adjacent to it. (This will help to keep the spirits in place and will make it seem as though they are holding hands.)

Craft 124: Gilded Heart

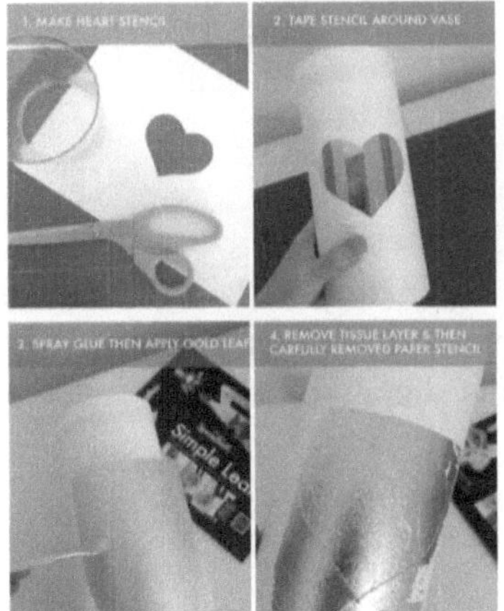

Materials

- Stencil material or firm card
- Gold leaf kit
- Craft knife or scissors
- A vase

- Spray glue

Directions

1. Make a stencil of a heart to use on your glass. Tape in place securely and then spray on the glue. Pat on the gold leaf and smooth it down. Peel off the tissue and stencil and you are done.

Craft 125: Heart on Your Sleeve Garland

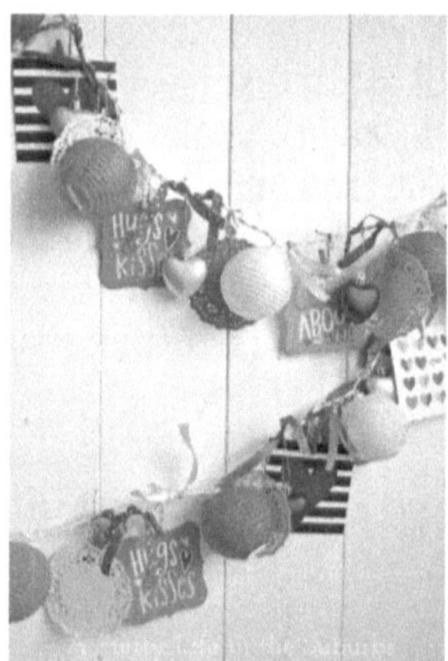

Materials

- Fairy lights with lantern covers
- Different décor items that will fit the theme (hearts, doilies, pretty ribbons, signs, valentine cards, etc.)
- Actual ornaments shaped like hearts
- A hole punch
- Bakers twine in pink or striped pink

Directions

1. Lay out all your decorations and punch holes in them if necessary. Lay them out in the order in which you want them to be hung. Using the baker's twine, attach the ornaments to the fairy lights. Add in some strips of ribbon. Continue until you have the desired effect. Then hang it up and switch it on.

Craft 126: Rustic Banner

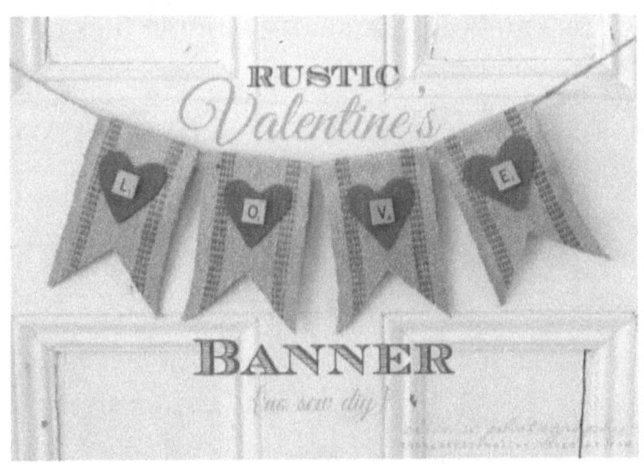

Materials

- Natural jute webbing (color stitched if possible)
- Nice red felt
- Scrabble tiles to make the word "love" a few times
- Natural jute string
- A hot glue gun

Directions

1. You will need four 7-inch strips of webbing, folded in half widthwise. Measure about two inches up the middle fold line and then cut diagonally from this point down to the opposite point. Repeat on the other side as well. Open the piece out again and now fold in half the other way. You should now have what looks like a pennant.

2. Next cut a length of the twine in the size that you need. Assemble the four banner pieces, ensuring that the jute is folded into the center. When you are happy with the spacing, glue the twine in place and glue the top of each pennant to the back of each one. If the fabric is curling in an unpleasant manner, it simply needs to be ironed.

3. Now you can decorate your banner. Start with cutting hearts out of the felt. (This is best accomplished by folding a heart template in half and placing this fold on the fold of your felt – that way you cut both sides of the heart out at once and save time and end up with a

more even effect. Glue one heart onto each pennant. To make it even more fun, glue on Scrabble letters that spell out the word "Love". (You can order packs of Scrabble tiles online)

Craft 127: Let Your Love Grow

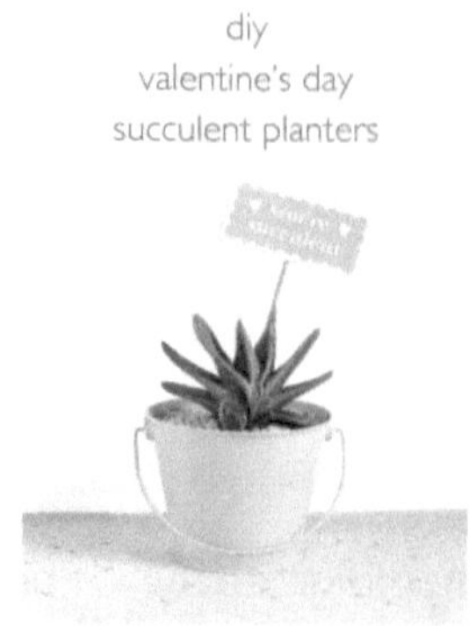

Materials

- Small little metal pails in pretty pastel colors
- Gravel for the fish tank (in white)
- Wooden skewers
- Some small cacti
- Appropriate sentiment tags (source online)
- A nail
- Rubber cement
- A hammer
- Soil suitable for the plan

Directions

1. Put the pail upside down and, using the hammer and nail, punch holes into the bottom of it to facilitate drainage. Put a layer of gravel at the bottom to help with more drainage and then half-fill the pot with soil. Plant the cactus, adding more soil as necessary, leaving enough room at the top of the pail to facilitate the addition of another layer of gravel. Water the plant and set aside. Print out an appropriate sentiment tag and attach to a skewer using the rubber cement. Place skewer in pail and the gift is ready.

Craft 128: Throw Your Heart Away

Materials

- A plain throw
- Fabric paint
- A large heart stamp
- A medium heart stamp
- A small heart stamp

Directions

1. Stamp hearts all over the throw. You can do the same as us and have a row of large hearts at the bottom with each successive layer getting smaller or you can make up your own mixed pattern. If it does not look right to you, a good wash should enable you to start over again. When the pattern is as you like it, touch up areas that need it using a small paint brush and set aside to dry. Heat set according to the manufacturer's recommendations and you are done.

Craft 129: Personalized Memory Box

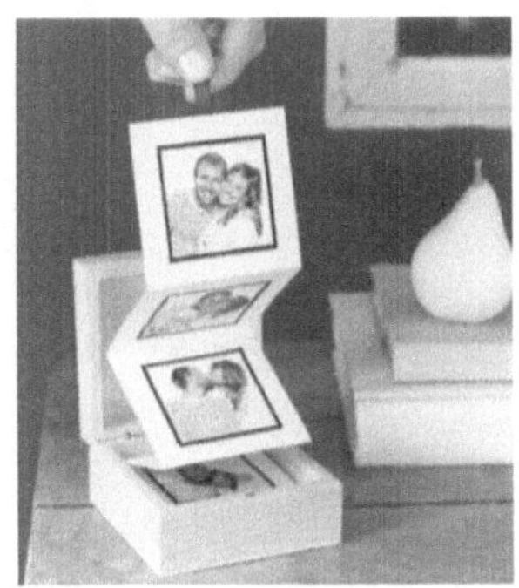

Materials

- A lidded wooden box (preferably square in shape)
- Meaningful photos (all cropped to the same size, in black and white. Use the box lid as a guide, you want the photos to be about a quarter inch smaller than the inside of the box lid on all sides)
- A long strip of firm card (it should be long enough to accommodate your photos in the box and should be just a little smaller than the inside of the box)
- Glue
- Scissors
- A piece of ribbon
- A bone folder or spoon

Directions

1. Start by ensuring that the card will fit well into the box. Accordion fold it so that it just fits in and is still easy to remove. Go over all the creases with your bone folder or spoon to ensure that they are sharp. Pull the accordion out of the box and choose which side your photos will be displayed on. Glue them on accordingly. Glue the underside of the card with the bottom photo into the box if you like. Fold all the cards back in, leaving a blank card on top. Cut a loop out of ribbon and attach to this card. Glue a second piece of card to hide ends and you are done.

Craft 130: Sweet Little Pincushion

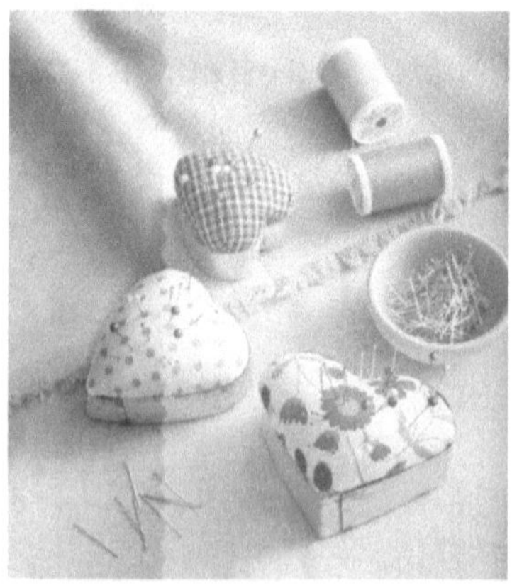

Materials

- Scrap bits of fabric
- Foam sheet
- Cookie cutters
- Hot glue
- Scissors
- Toy stuffing

Directions

1. Trace around your cookie cutter onto the foam to get the right size Cover the foam with scraps, making sure that the bottom is nice and smooth – the top will not be seen anyway. Cut a second piece of fabric that will be able to fit over the top of the cookie cutter, with room to spare for the stuffing. Glue three sides of this down onto the sides of the foam, stuff well and glue down the fourth side. Push the shape into the cookie cutter and your pincushion is done.

Craft 131: Lovely Window Art

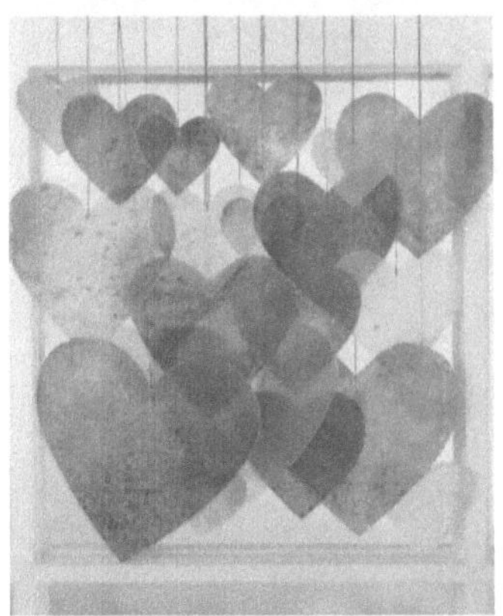

Materials

- Waxed paper
- Crayons
- A pencil sharpener
- Construction paper
- An iron

- A pencil
- Thread
- Scissors

Directions

1. Start off by taking a sheet of wax paper and fold it in half lengthwise. Sharpen the crayons and collect the shavings on one half of the paper. This should be an even, thin layer. Fold the clean paper over and seal the edges with more folds.

2. Put the construction paper on your ironing board to protect it. Put the waxed paper on top of this and then add another sheet of construction paper. Iron over a medium heat, just long enough to melt the shavings. (Make sure that the steam setting is off.) Leave to cool off. Trace out the heart shapes and cut them out. String them up with the thread.

Craft 132: Glittered Candle

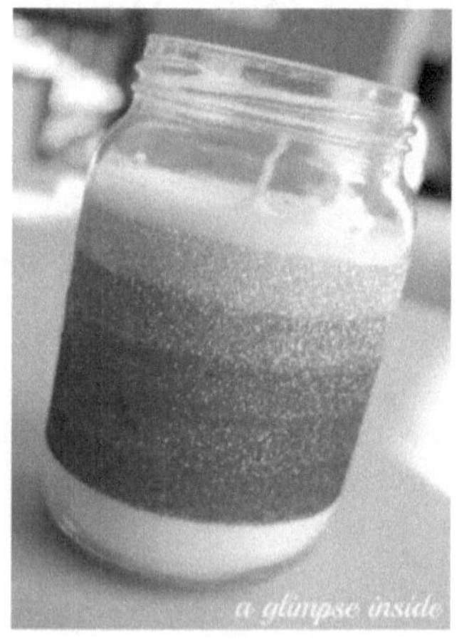

Materials

- A candle of your choice with smooth sides or one in a glass
- Glitter in several different colors
- Some double-sided tape
- Wax paper

Directions

1. Make sure that there is no type of residue on the outside of your glass. Wrap your double-sided tape all around the jar starting at the bottom and working your way up. Stop where you want your first line to start. Keep the wrapping even and overlapping a little. Remove the first line of adhesive tape cover and sprinkle your first color glitter over it, ensuring that it is well covered. Shake off excess and move on to the next row, repeat until all the lines are done. Wipe off excess glitter on the candle/ bottle and you are done.

Craft 133: Valentine's Day Earrings

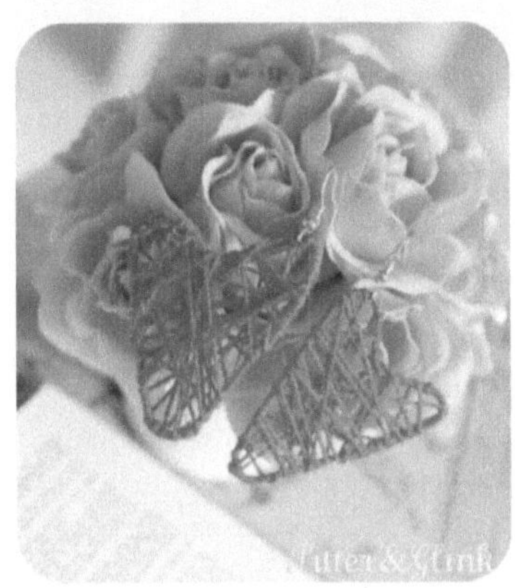

Materials

- Two paper clips (red)
- String n red
- Liquid stitch
- Earring hooks

Directions

1. Start by opening out the paper clip until you get a rough heart shape. Knot the string onto the bottom of the heart and secure with the glue. When dry, wind the string all around the paper clip so that the whole clip is covered. When you get to the ends of the clip, tie them together and wrap to stabilize. Once the metal is all covered, drape sting across the whole heart, securing with glue as

necessary. When you have the effect that you want, attach the earring hooks.

Craft 134: Candle Garland

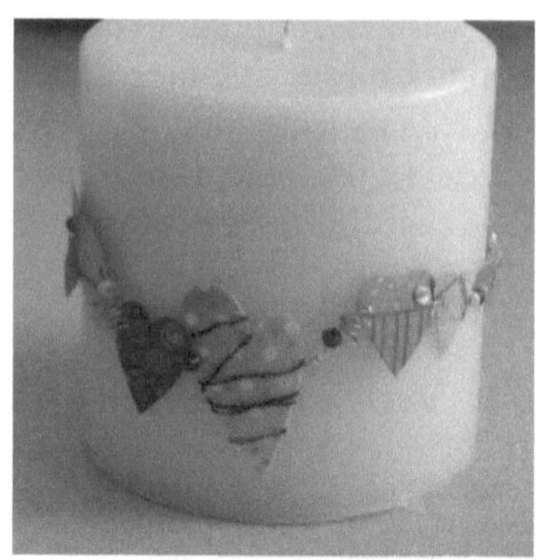

Materials

- 1 white pillar candle
- An assortment of beads
- 22 gauge craft wire
- A dowel with a circumference of a quarter inch
- Pretty patterned card stock
- A heart punch or templates in different sizes
- Stickers appropriate to the project
- Scrap card in plain colors
- Fine-tipped pens
- Rhinestones to match
- Some matching embroidery cotton
- Elmer's Glue
- A hat pin

Directions

1. Measure the entire circumference of the candle and cut the wire so that it will be long enough to go around the candle twice. Put to one side. Punch or cut a few different hearts from the card stock and decorate with rhinestones, pens, embroidery cotton, etc. Leave some hearts just plain as they are.

2. Put your heart stickers onto plain card stock and then cut them out. Make a small hole on either side of the hearts that you can use to thread the wire through. Intersperse the hearts with beads. Every now and again, coil the wire with the dowel or create a zig zag. Leave the last inch on either side of the wire free so that you can tie it off at the back when you are done. Coil the excess wire to hide the join.

Craft 135: Valentine's Wreath

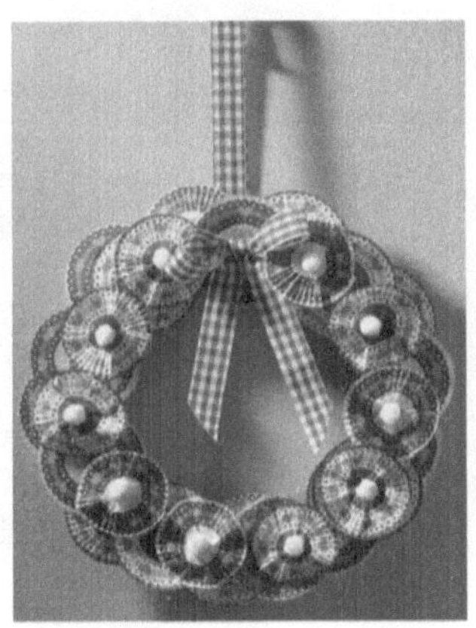

Materials

- A wreath base
- Cupcake wrappers in red and white
- 9″ sheet of plain craft foam (thick-cut)
- A crepe paper roll in red
- Roll red crepe paper
- 10 little white pom-poms
- About a meter of gingham ribbon in red and white
- A hot glue gun
- Scissors
- Straight pins

Directions

1. Cover the entire wreath with the crepe paper and glue securely at the back. Wrap a length of ribbon at the very apex of the wreath so that you have something to hang it from. Glue into place. Flatten

each of the cupcake wrappers and glue into place on wreath, covering the whole surface. Cut small squares of foam and glue them to the back of some other wrappers. Scrunch these wrappers slightly so they have more body and then glue a pom-pom into each front center of these wrappers. Glue these wrappers in place on the wreath.

Craft 136: A Cute Message

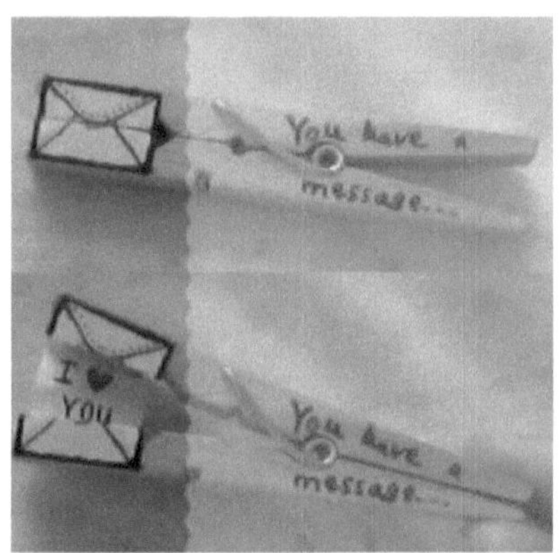

Materials

- A few pencils
- Some colored fine-tip pens
- A permanent marker with a fine tip
- Glue
- Clothespins
- Scissors

Directions

1. Write a small message on the clothespin itself – something like "you have mail". Draw on an envelope on the "teeth" of the clothespin. You will need to get a piece of paper that is at least double the height of your envelope. Accordion fold it so that you have two ends to attach to the peg and a space in the center for your message. Write your message and glue it to the back of the peg. When someone opens the peg, they will see your message.

Craft 137: Heart Shaped Garnish

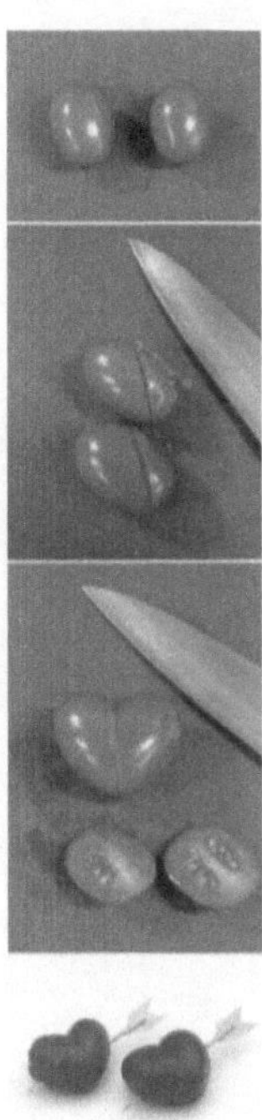

Materials

- Small rosa tomatoes
- A sharp knife
- Toothpicks
- An arrow printable
- Glue

Directions

1. The art to this craft is to cut the tomatoes properly. Find the halfway point of your tomatoes and make a cut from there to the other side at a 45-degree angle. Do the same with a second tomato and place the two cut sides together to form a heart. Hold the heart together with a toothpick and glue on some arrow printables so that it looks as though the heart has an arrow through it.

Craft 138: Mason Jar Valentine's Day Craft

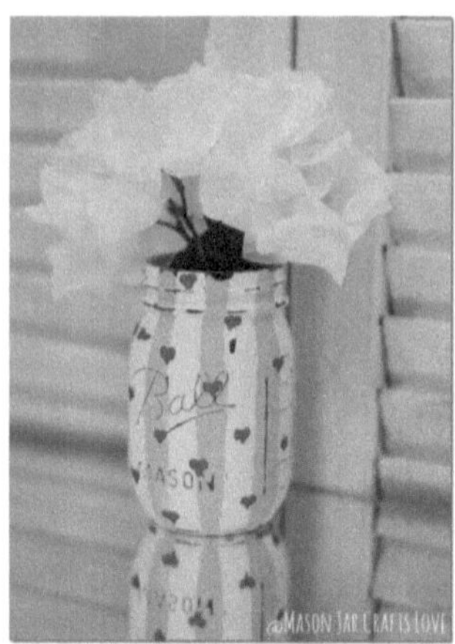

Materials

- Chalk paint
- Mason jars
- Washi tape
- Modge Podge
- A sponge brush
- A small paint brush
- A fine sandpaper

Directions

1. Start off by painting each of the jars with a coat of Modge Podge for better adhesion. When this is dry, continue with your primary colors and set aside to dry. Apply a second coat in need and leave to dry. Mark out where you want your stripes to be and put washi tape over the other areas. Paint on the color for your stripes and leave to dry.

2. Remove the tape and touch up any areas that need it. Lightly sand the surface every now and again to create a distressed look. Then paint on the hearts. This is easiest done if you paint them as a series of three dots each to get the basic shape right.

Craft 139: Clay Hearts

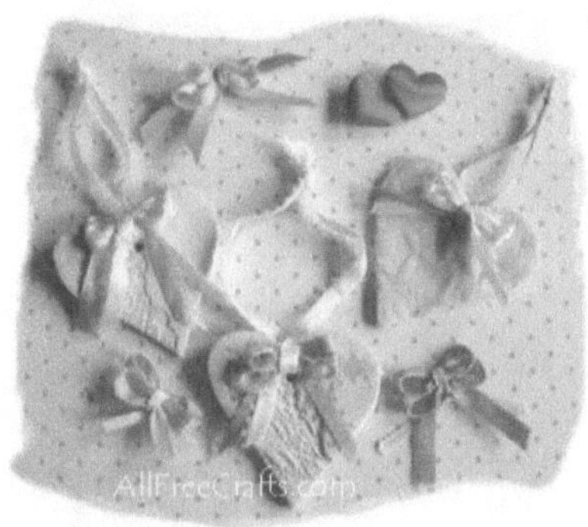

Materials

- Polymer clay that can be cured in the oven or air-dry clay
- A sturdy rolling pin
- A cookie cutter in the shape of a heart
- A knife
- A plate
- A wooden skewer
- A ceramic tile to cut on
- Adhesive tape
- Acrylic paint (optional)
- Varnish to seal
- Lace (to create an imprinted pattern)
- Ribbon

Directions

1. Roll out the clay until about a quarter of an inch thick. Cut out the hearts using your cookie cutter. Make a hole in the top of the heart using your skewer that the ribbon can fit through.

2. Bring out the items that you want to imprint with texture and press them into the clay. (Rubber stamps work quite well, as do lace doilies, door handles, buttons, etc.). Either bake the hearts or leave them to cure according to the manufacturer's instructions. You can, if you like, paint the hearts as well or coat with a clear varnish.

Craft 140: Baring Your Heart

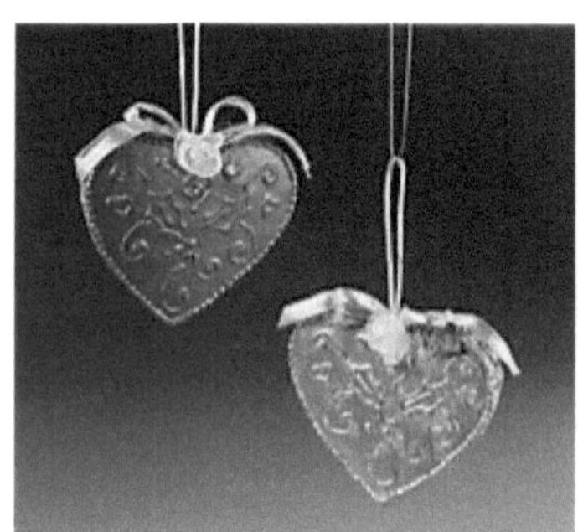

Materials

- A foam heart
- Craft foam
- A faux finish paint
- Textured paint or hot glue
- A squeeze bottle with a narrow tip to help with intricate designs
- Wire edged organza ribbon in silver
- An organza ribbon rose
- Silver colored cord to hang the ornament with
- A toothpick
- A palette knife or something similar
- A foam brush
- A ceramic tile
- Paper towels
- Water
- Scissors

Directions

1. Thread the heart onto a toothpick but do not let it go all the way through to allow you to apply your textured paint in the pattern that you want. Alternatively, you can also make your patterns at this stage using your hot glue gun. Leave to dry before applying the faux finish.

2. Knot the cord so that you have a loop and hide the knot you made in the hole made by the toothpick. Glue into position. Make a bow

from the organza ribbon and glue it and the organza rose to the top of the heart.

Craft 141: Love and Kisses

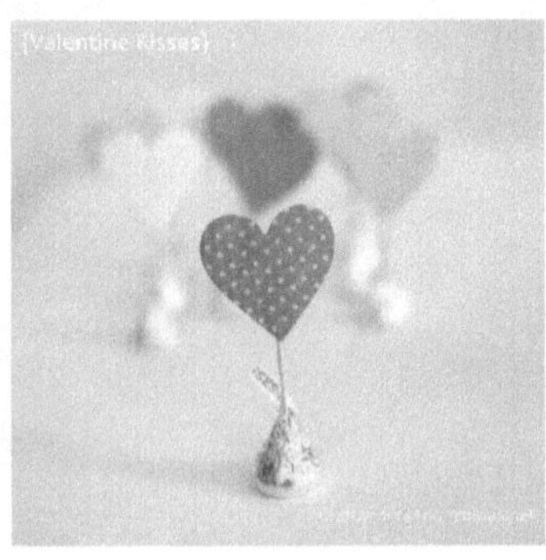

Materials

- Hershey's kisses (still wrapped)
- Pretty paper hearts
- Toothpicks
- Glue

Directions

1. Each kiss will require two hearts. Glue two hearts together, right side facing out with the toothpick in between them. Insert into the Hershey's kiss and you are done.

Craft 142: Heart Garland

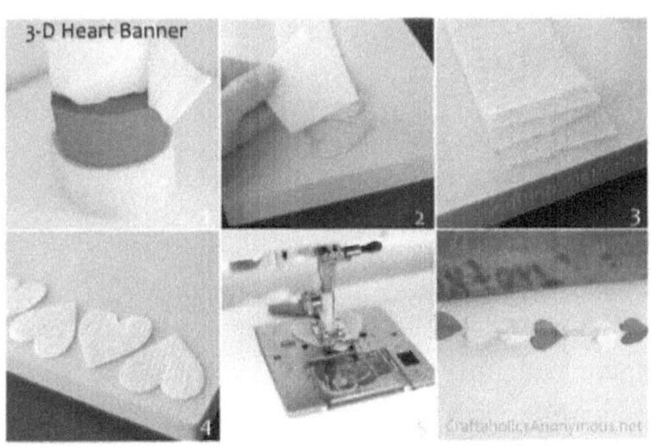

Materials

- Rolls of crepe streamers
- A heart die
- A die cutting machine
- A sewing machine
- Thread

Directions

1. Lay out at least 4 layers of crepe paper over the die and put through the die cutting machine. Take the first set of four hearts and make a running stitch across the center on your sewing machine. Do not break the thread and then sew the next heart so that you eventually end up with a long banner. Finish off by fluffing out the hearts.

Craft 143: Bold Valentine's Wreath

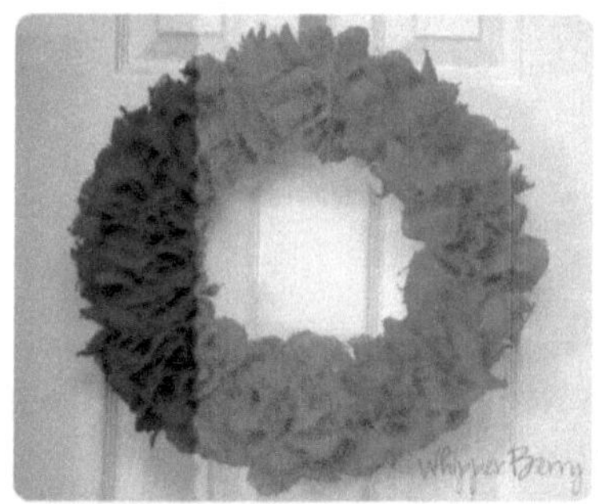

Materials

- Red burlap
- A wreath base
- A hot glue gun
- Paint in a matching color

Directions

1. Paint the base red and set aside to dry. Cut the burlap into squares of 5 inches each. Squirting some water onto the burlap will go a long way to help deal with the mess. Fold the burlap in half twice

and then round off the top open corner so that when it opens out it looks roughly like a flower. Scrunch each flower up in the center and hot glue onto the wreath base. Continue until you get the fullness that you want.

Craft 144: Contemporary Heart Decoration

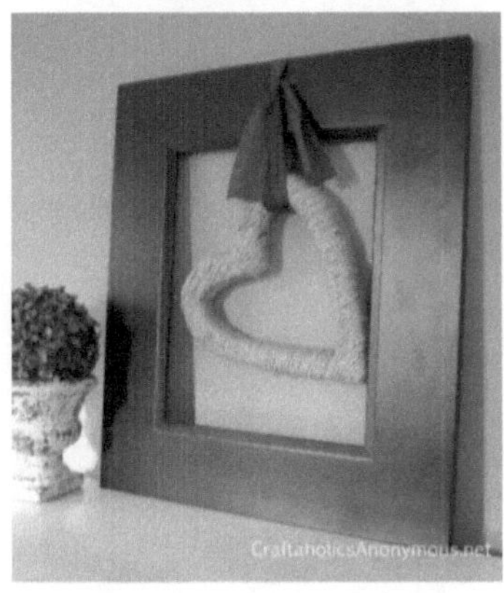

Materials

- A wooden heart form
- Padding (optional)
- Natural twine
- A frame that the heart will fit into
- Ribbon
- Glue

Directions

1. Glue some padding onto the heart in an even layer if you are using it. Wrap the heart in the twine, ensuring that no gaps appear and secure every now and again with glue. Secure the ends of the twine at the back of the heart with glue.

2. Remove the glass and backing from the frame and set aside. If you would like to, you can paint the frame. Once the frame is ready, thread the ribbon through the heart and attach loosely to the frame by tying a knot in it.

Craft 145: Yarn Wreath

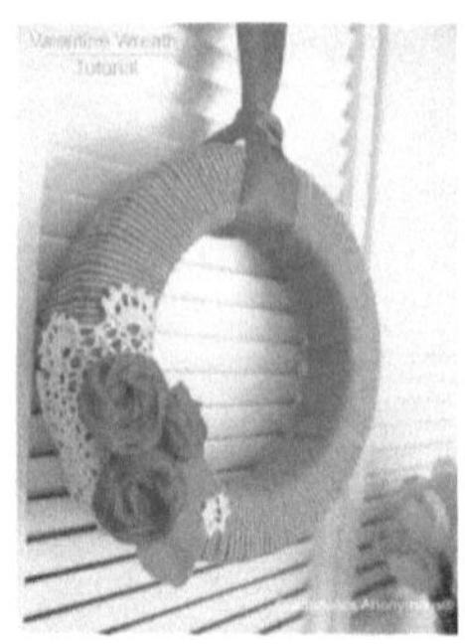

Materials

- A wreath base
- Yarn of your choice
- Oddments of lace
- Felt flowers and leaves
- A hot glue gun

Directions

1. Wrap the yarn carefully around the wreath base, if you are using two different colors, hot glue the ends down and then run them simultaneously around the base until the whole thing is covered. Wrap your oddments of lace around the base, with the cut sides at the back and glue into place. Create a spray of flowers and leaves and hot glue that into place as well.

Craft 146: Contemporary Valentine's Wreath

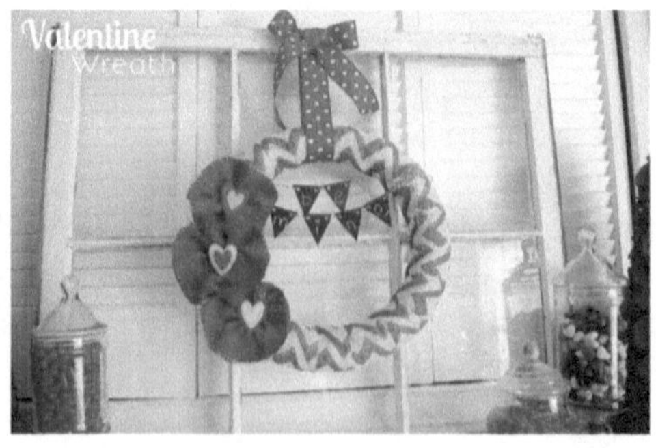

Materials

- Chevron printed burlap
- A bright red burlap
- Felt hearts in white and red
- A striking ribbon to hang it with
- A printable bunting banner
- A wreath base
- A hot glue gun
- Baker's twine

Directions

1. Start by wrapping the chevron printed burlap around the wreath base until it is completely covered. Hot glue into place. Cut a few circles out of the red burlap, put a dollop of glue in the center and scrunch up the bases slightly so that it looks more like a flower. (Don't touch the glue itself, it will be hot.)

2. Write your message on the printed bunting and string it up using baker's twine. Tie onto the right side of the wreath with a pretty bow. Tie on the other side securely. Using the flowers that you created in the step above, cover the one end of the baker's twine. Glue felt hearts into the center. Finish off by threading the bold ribbon through the center and closing the loop with a bow.

Craft 147: Natural Thanksgiving Wreath

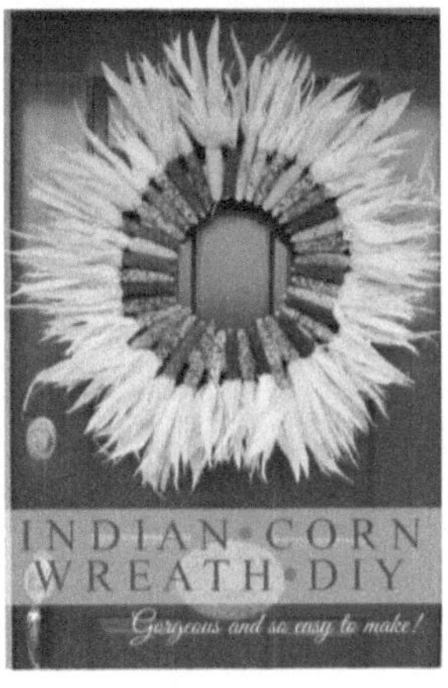

Materials

- Mini cobs of Indian corn with husks in place
- A straw wreath base
- A hot glue gun

Directions

1. Fluff each of the corn husks out properly. Hot-glue each corn ear onto the wreath, making sure that there are no gaps in between.

Craft 148: Great Thanksgiving Wreath

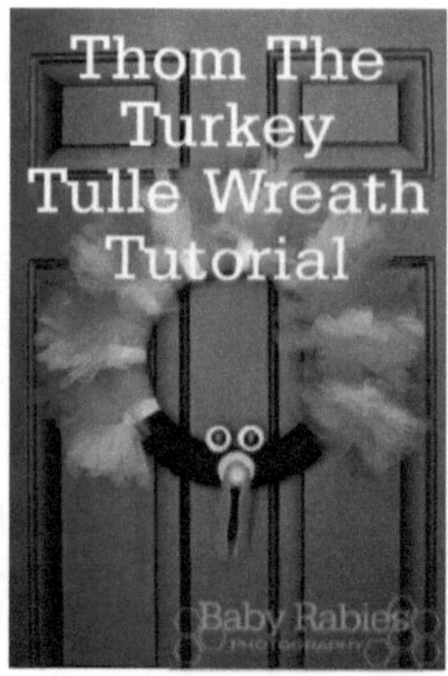

Materials

- 2 ping pong balls
- 1 little cone that can be used as a beak
- A wreath base
- A spool of tulle in the color of your choice (or two different colors if you like)
- A ball of brown yarn
- Craft foam in red
- Acrylic paint in black and yellow
- A paint brush
- A hot glue gun

1. Paint the cone yellow and paint black circles on the ping pong balls so that they look like eyes. Put them aside so that they can dry. Wrap the bottom third of the wreath base with the yarn, making sure that no base shows through. This will form the turkey's body. Tie securely and trim the ends.

2. You will need about 15 tulle strips in all. The easiest way to cut them evenly is to wrap your tulle around a box or piece of stiff card and then to just cut the closed edges – as if you were making a pom-pom. Tie each piece of tulle onto the wreath to create the feathers, ensuring that the rest of the base is covered. You can now glue the eyes and beak onto the body of the turkey.

3. The last step is to fold your foam into equal halves and to make the turkey's waddle. This should get wider at the ends and be fairly narrow at the top. Glue this in place over the beak.

Craft 149: Turkey Gobblers

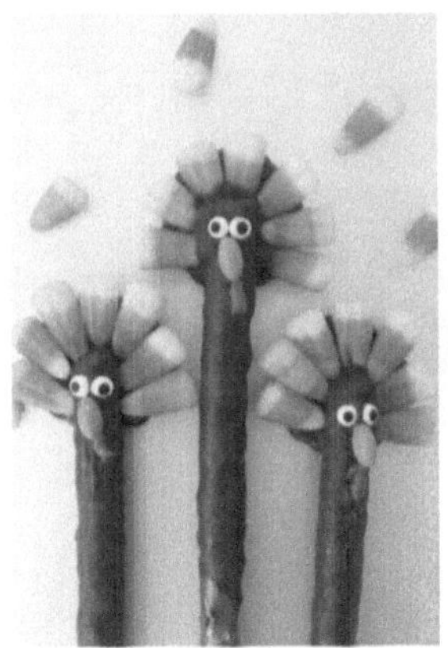

Materials

- 12 Straight pretzels
- 12 cookies covered in chocolate
- 24 edible eyes
- 84 Candy corns
- 12 Reese's pieces, orange

- 125ml milk cooking chocolate
- 35ml red easy (melt candy)
- Non-stick baking paper
- A cookie tin

Directions

1. Line the baking tin with baking paper and set out each cookie. You need to leave at least 5cm space on all sides of the cookies. In need, use a second baking tin. Place a pretzel in the center or each cookie to form the body of the turkey.

2. Melt the chocolate in the microwave according to directions and then use as a "glue" for the candy corns. Arrange seven candy corns on each cookie and "glue" in place. Remove the pretzel and dip half-way in the melted chocolate before adhering to the center of the cookie again. "Glue" on the eyes and use a bit of the orange Reese's to make the beak. Put the red candy into a plastic bag and microwave for about 30 seconds. Clip the corner off the bag and pipe the candy on as the turkey's waddle. Set aside to set and you are done.

Craft 150: Pilgrim Party Favors

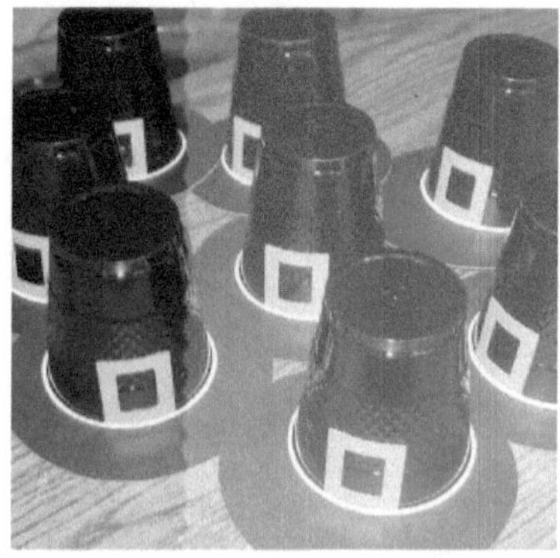

Materials

- Plastic cups (if possible, black. If you cannot find black cups, paint white ones)
- Strips of white paper (optional)

- Heavy card in black and yellow
- Glue
- Scissors

Directions

1. Cut circles that are a good size to be the brim of your hat out of the black card. Cut a buckle out of the yellow card and glue onto the cup. The next part needs to be done quickly. Dispense some glue onto a saucer big enough to fit the rim of the cup into it. Dip the rim of the cup into the glue and then quickly fill the cup with sweets. Before the glue dries, snap on the black card brim. And set aside to dry.

Craft 151: Horn of Plenty

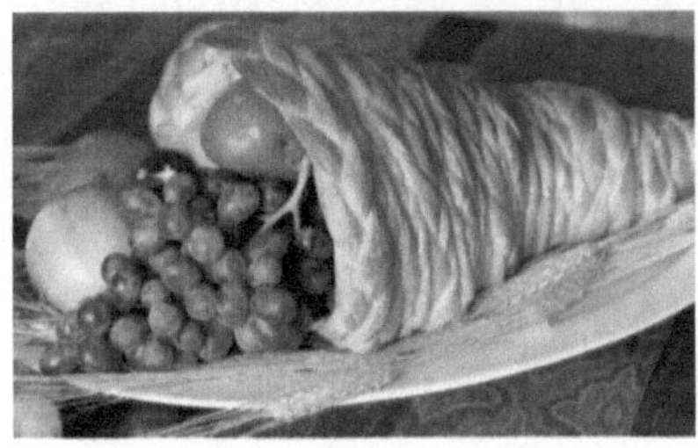

Materials

- Bread dough
- Heavy duty foil
- A water bottle/cone to use as a template
- An egg
- Water
- Baking spray

Directions

1. Wrap the template in the foil so that you have a giant cone of foil once you are done. You will need to have at least four layers to ensure that the cone will support the weight of the bread dough. When you think that you have enough layers, fold the edges around the wide end of the cone so that they are straight and so that there is even more support where it is needed. Smooth out the

foil and take out the template. Smooth the sides of the foil as well and curl the tail a little.

2. Now it is time to pack on the dough. Bread dough is best but pizza dough will also work. Roll the dough out into a flat rectangular sheet about a half inch in thickness. Cut the dough into strips measuring one-inch wide. Spray the foil with copious amounts of baking spray and then lay the strips onto this, starting at the thinnest end and working your way towards the widest end. The strips should overlap each other a little. Leave about an inch of space at the opening of the cone so that you can more easily get the foil out.

3. For a braided rim, you will need to take three of these strips and braid them and then secure them to the rim of the cornucopia. Beat an egg and a little water together and use as a wash for the dough. Bake at 350F for between twenty and forty minutes or until nice and golden brown.

Craft 152: Acorn Kisses

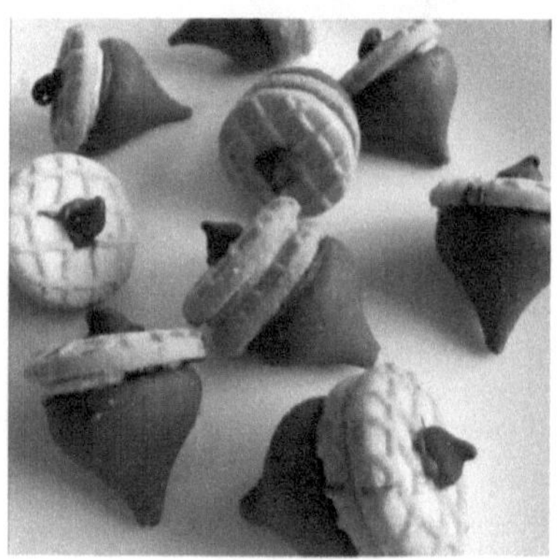

Materials

- Easy melt milk chocolate
- Hershey's kisses
- Bite-sized biscuits of your choosing
- Chocolate chips

Directions

1. Melt the chocolate in the microwave according to the manufacturer'
    instructions. Dip the base of the Hershey's Kiss into the chocolate
    and use this to stick it to the biscuit. Flip the biscuit over and dip
    the base of a chocolate chip in the chocolate to adhere it to the
    other side as the acorn stem.

Craft 153: Rustic Thanksgiving Bunting

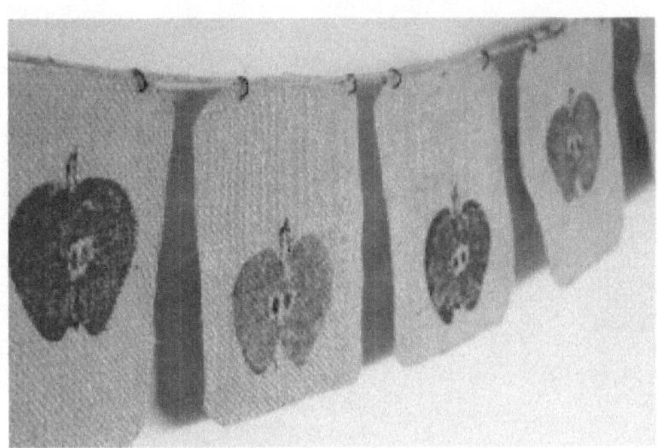

Materials

-   Old burlap bags
-   Fabric paint
-   An apple for each color
-   A paint brush
-   Twine
-   Jump rings
-   A glazed ceramic tile
-   Markers that will write on burlap

Directions

1. Cut the sacks up into evenly sized rectangular pieces. Cut each
    apple in half and drop some paint on the tile. Spread it out and use
    the apple as a stamp. Each banner can be a different color or the
    same as you like. Set the pieces aside to dry. Once dry, fill in the
    details with the marker as required. Using the jump rings, hang the
    pieces on the twine.

Craft 154: Glittery Leaf Bunting

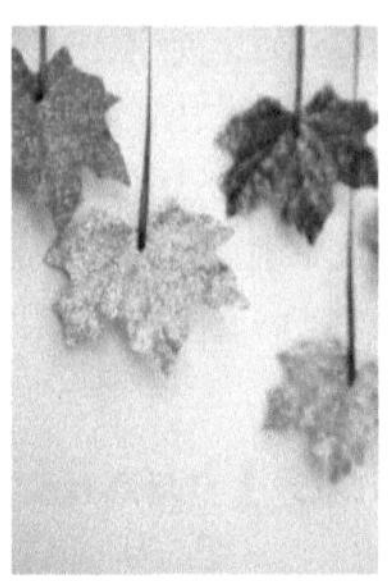

Materials

- Craft leaves
- Elmer's glue
- Glitter
- A hole punch
- Ribbon

Directions

1. Apply a thin coat of the glue to one leaf at a time. Sprinkle glitter on so that it is thickly coated and leave to dry. Shake the excess glitter off. Make a hole in the top area of the leaf and strand the ribbon through it. Tie the individual ribbons to a matching long strand and your bunting is done.

Craft 155: Gratitude Board

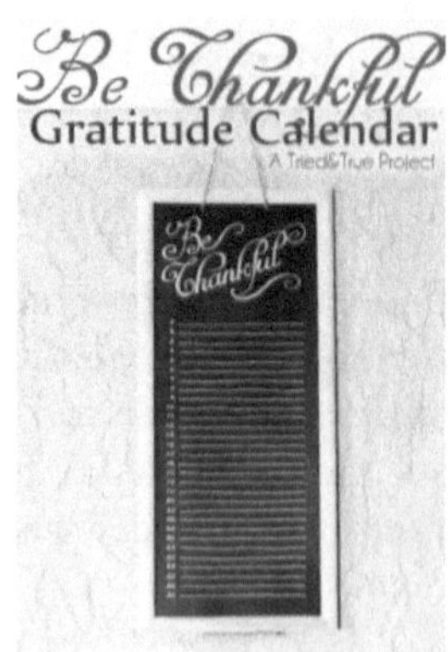

Materials

- A plain chalkboard, longer than it is wide, framed
- A white chalk pen
- A sheet of transfer paper
- A print of the text you want to use
- A pencil
- A ruler
- Paper towel

Directions

1. Put your transfer paper up against the chalkboard and lay your printout on top of that. Tape in place and then trace the letters onto the board using even pressure. Go over areas you are not sure that you got to. Remove the transfer paper and text.

2. Go over the traced lines with your chalk pen and color as applicable. Using a ruler, draw the lines in on the board so that you have space to write what you are grateful for being sure to wipe the ruler clean each time so that the lines do not smudge.

Craft 156: Leaf Bowl

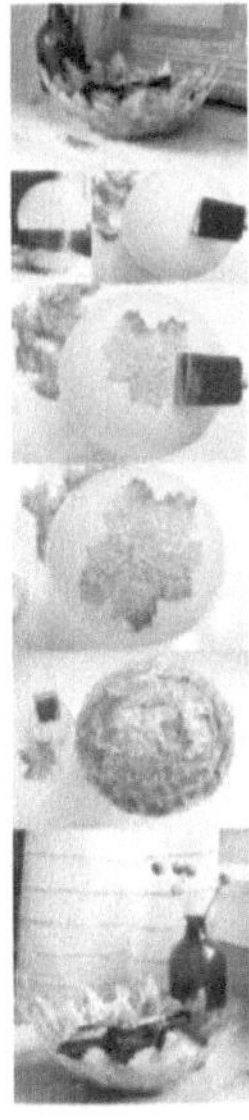

Materials

- Elmer's glue
- A sponge brush
- Fall leaves from the garden
- A balloon

Directions

1. Blow up the balloon to an appropriate size. Cover the top of the balloon with glue and then start to put your leaves in place. Carry on until the bowl is the size that you want it to be, each time, putting lots of glue over the leaves. Place a second and third layer of leaves so that the bowl is even sturdier and set everything aside so that it can dry undisturbed. You will need to let it cure for at least two – three days, or, if possible, a week to be on the safe side. Once dry, pop the balloon and peel off any remnants of plastic.

Craft 157: Votives For Your Table

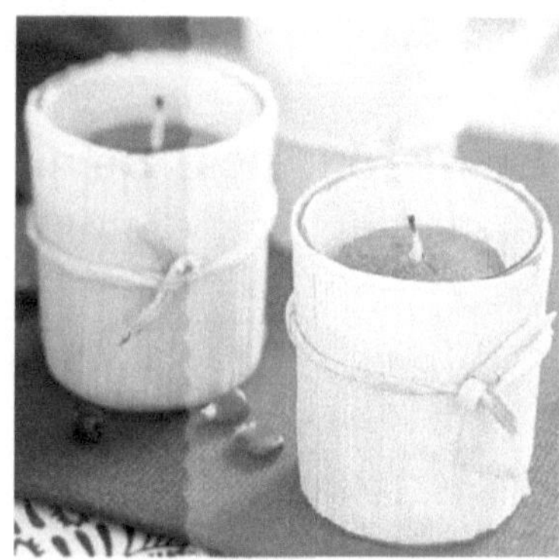

Materials

- Medium sized votive glasses
- Husks for making tamales
- An elastic band

Directions

1. This is an easy one. Soak the husks in a bowl of warm, not boiling water, for about two minutes. They are ready when they are

flexible. Wrap one of the husks around each votive glass and secure with an elastic band. Break one of the husks into strips and tie a strip around each votive glass. You can now remove the elastic band and set aside to dry. Once dry, carefully cut away any excess.

Craft 158: Very Berry Wreath

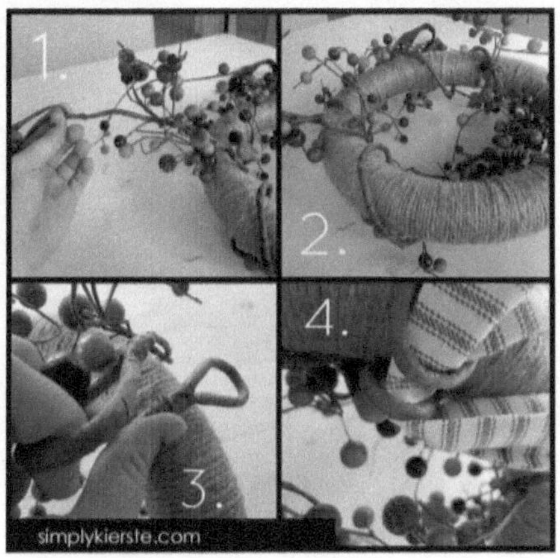

Materials

- A wreath base
- Natural twine or jute
- A garland of berries
- A matching roll of ribbon
- A hot glue gun

Directions

1. Wrap the wreath base with the twine tightly, ensuring that there are no gaps. Glue to the base every now and then and secure the ends with hot glue. Wrap the garland of berries around the wreath base and secure in place using hot glue as necessary. You must ensure that both of the "handles" of the garland are lined up at the end. Pass your length of ribbon through the garland ends and tie a huge bow in it to cover up the garland ends.

Craft 159: Fall Table Rings

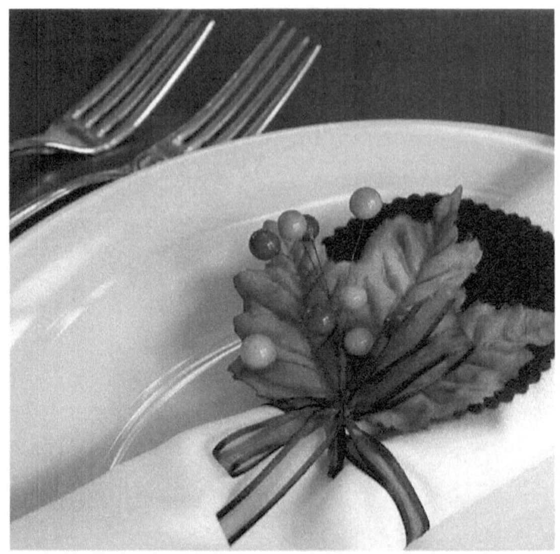

Materials

- Craft leaves (or use real fall leaves if you like)
- Craft berry sprays
- Felt
- Pinking shears
- Ribbon
- A hot glue gun

Directions

1. Cut a 3-inch circle from the felt using your pinking shears. Glue this to the base of the leaf – you want some of the stem to be hanging off the side and none of the circle to be seen. Wrap the berry sprays onto the stem of the leaf and add a dab of glue.

2. Cut your ribbon into 24-inch pieces, seal the ends and fold each piece in half. Place the leaf stem at the center and tie the ribbon around this, adding a dab of glue as necessary. When you are ready to use it, simply tie the ribbon in a bow around the napkin.

Craft 160: Upcycled Bottle Thanksgiving Craft

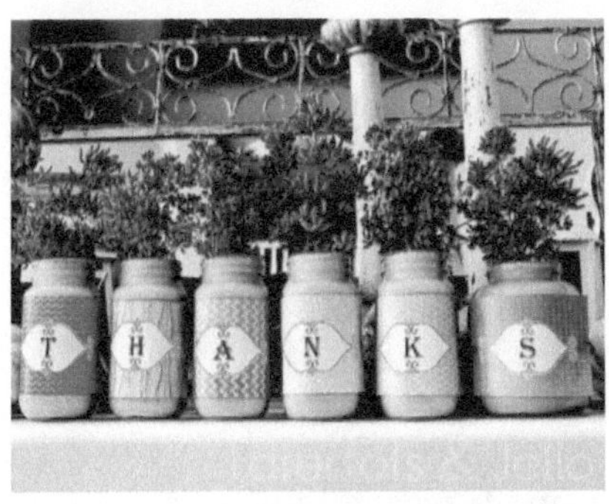

Materials

- 6 old food jars, cleaned thoroughly
- Pretty scrapbook paper
- Paint
- A printable label template

Directions

1. Pour a little paint into the bottom of each jar and swirl it around until the whole. Cut a band of scrapbooking paper that will fit around the body of the bottle and secure using a little bit of adhesive tape at the back where no one will see it. Find a label template online and print out one letter of the word "Thanks" on each of them. Stick these to the middle of the scrapbooking paper.

Craft 161: Fall Votive

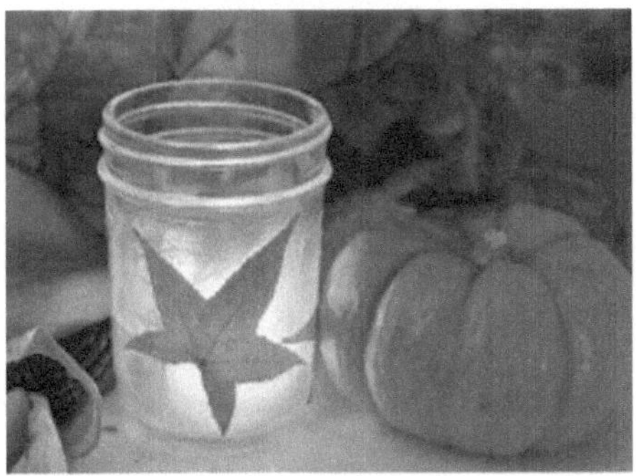

Materials

- Fall leaves from the garden
- Modge Podge
- A foam brush
- Votive glasses or old jam jars

Directions

1. Apply a layer of Modge Podge to the outside of the votive glass or jar and stick your leaves down. Apply two coats of Modge Podge over the top of the leaves, allowing each to dry before applying the next.

Craft 162: Elegant Pumpkin Centerpiece

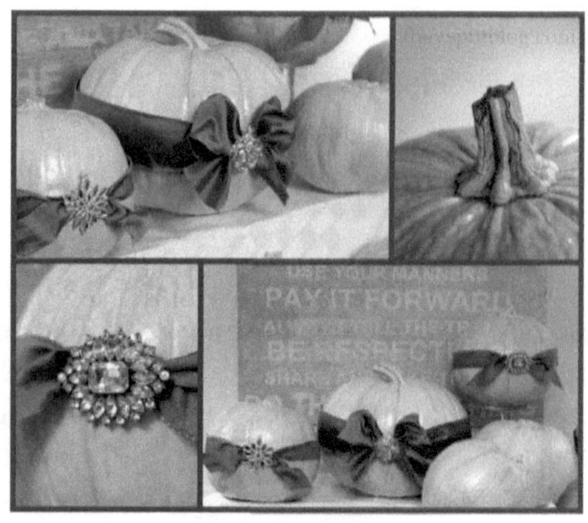

Materials

- Spray paint in an off-white color
- Olive green acrylic paint
- Pearlized paint
- Spray on varnish
- Ribbon
- Glitzy buckle or vintage brooch
- Floral pins

Directions

1. Spray the pumpkin with the spray paint and set aside to dry. Once dry, take your olive green and paint a fine line in the grooves of the pumpkin. Do one line at a time and immediately go over these with a wider brush dipped in water to help blend in the lines. Then paint on a thin wash of the pearlized paint over the bulges of the pumpkin and set aside to dry.

2. Once dry, wrap a length of ribbon around your pumpkin – you have two options, to end it off with a huge bow or to simply just cross the ends of the ribbon together at the front and pin them into place. Up the wow factor by adding on a glitzy old brooch of vintage buckle and keeping it in place with floral pins.

Craft 163: Thanks for The Pumpkin

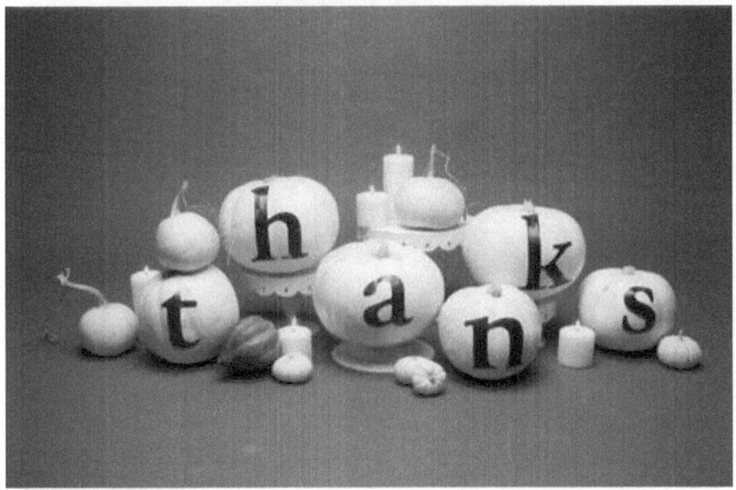

Materials

- 6 pumpkins, around about the same size
- White spray paint
- Black paint
- Letter stencils
- Spray varnish (optional)

Directions

1. Spray paint the pumpkins lightly with the white paint and set aside to dry. When dry tape the stencil to the pumpkin and paint in the letters with the black paint. Remove letters and leave to dry. Finish off with a coat of spray varnish.

Craft 164: Pilgrim's Pot

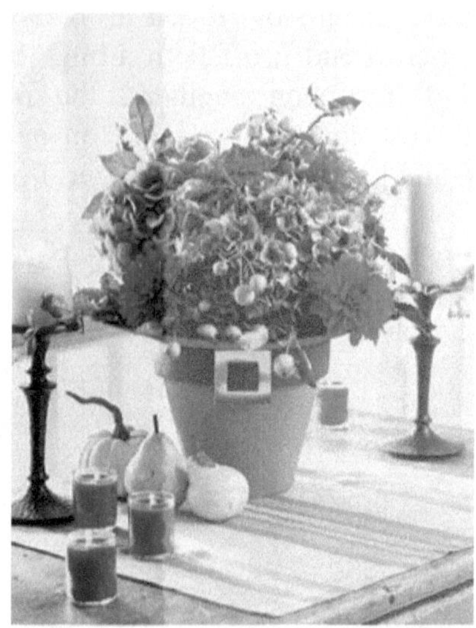

Materials

- A terracotta pot
- A dark brown leather or velvet ribbon strip
- A craft knife or scissors
- A hot glue gun
- Scissors or craft knife
- Gold paper with a metallic finish or a small buckle

Directions

1. Trim the strip to match the brim of the pot and make it a little wider. Glue into place using the glue gun. Cut the buckle out of the gold paper and glue that on as well.

Craft 165: Dashing Wreath

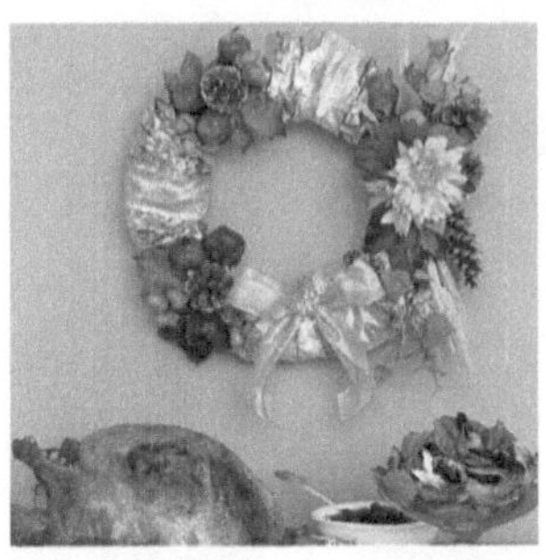

Materials

- Scissors
- 12 to 14 paper bags (lunch bags in brown are best)
- A length of foil (gold in color)
- A wreath base
- Gaffers tape
- A gold-colored permanent marker
- Fall decorations of your choice
- A hot glue gun

Directions

1. Slice off the bag bottoms and slit the sides so that the bags are a long flat strip. Cut these into strips of around 4 inches in width. Twist each strip a little and then crumple slightly. Now cut 3 lengths of foil, each around 18 inches in length and then cut these into long strips as you did the brown paper. Repeat the twisting and crumpling.

2. Wrap your strips of brown paper around the wreath base, ensuring that you get even coverage and that none of the base shows through. Glue into place at regular intervals on the bag. Glue when done. Repeat this process with the gold strips as well. Now you can start adding on whatever decorations you found. You can use the marker to add a bit of glitz to your decorations if you like – paint the tips of the pinecones or maybe the acorns – it is your wreath, you choose. Build up your decorations in layers and position as you like them. Hot glue into place.

Craft 166: Golden Wheat Decoration

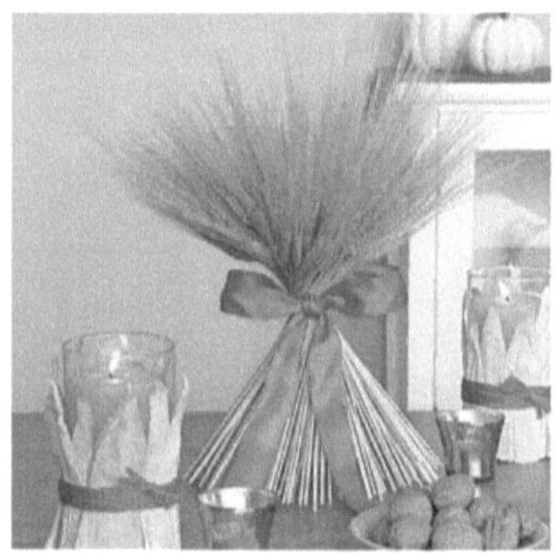

Materials

- About 24 ounces of wheat sheaves
- Scissors
- 2 Twist ties
- Wide ribbon to match your décor

Directions

1. Grab a handful of wheat and check that all the stems are about the same size – remove those that are too short and discard. Those that are too long can be trimmed as required. Split the remaining wheat into two equal sections, one in each hand. Gently fan out the wheat until you get the desired effect. Secure with twist ties, around the thinnest middle section – about where your hands are. Tie a large bow onto the sheaf to hide the twist tie.

Craft 167: Table Centerpiece

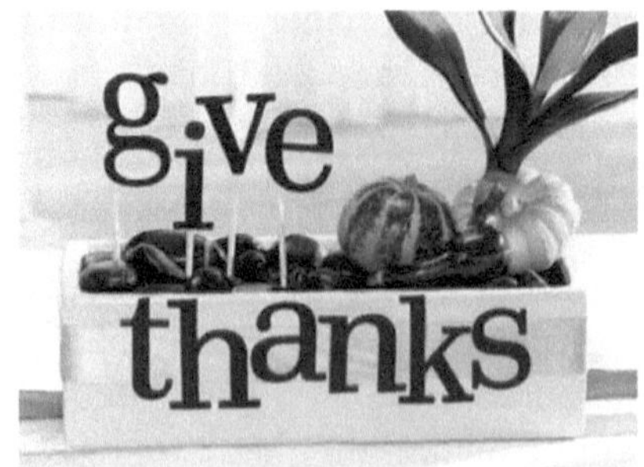

Materials

- A long rectangular planter
- Enough floral foam to cover the inside (color doesn't matter)
- Black (smooth pebbles from the river)
- 4 lollipop sticks in white
- Pre-cut letters in black that say "give thanks"
- Gourds or pumpkins of your choice
- Artificial greenery
- Wide satin ribbon to match your decor
- A hot glue gun
- Adhesive tape

Directions

1. Place the floral foam in the planter and trim as needed. You need to leave about an inch between the foam top and the rim of the planter. Cover the whole surface with your pebbles. On the right hand side of the planter, arrange your greenery and secure in the florist's foam. Add the gourds/ pumpkins here.

2. Now you can wind your ribbon around the planter to create a decorative effect. Secure with either hot glue or adhesive tape. Take the letters that say "Thanks" and glue them onto the ribbon strip. Put a dab of hot glue on the back of the rest of the letters and affix the lollipop sticks. When dry, place in the foam and you are done.

Craft 168: Light Up Your Thanksgiving

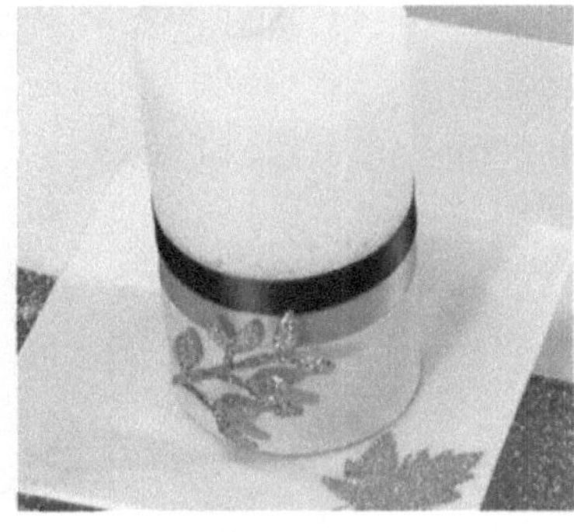

Materials

- A tall, fat pillar candle in white
- 1 Inch wide satin ribbon in two complimentary colors
- Pretty paper that will also match in
- A glittered leaf spray (optional)
- A hot glue gun

Directions

1. Cover the bottom half of the candle with a strip of the pretty paper and glue into place. Then disguise the cut edge by overlapping the first strip of ribbon over it. Glue into place. Place the second strip of ribbon just above this, slightly overlapping the first piece and glue into place. If you are using the leaf spray, glue in place now. Glue on any other embellishments that you feel might be necessary.

Craft 169: Contemporary Centerpiece

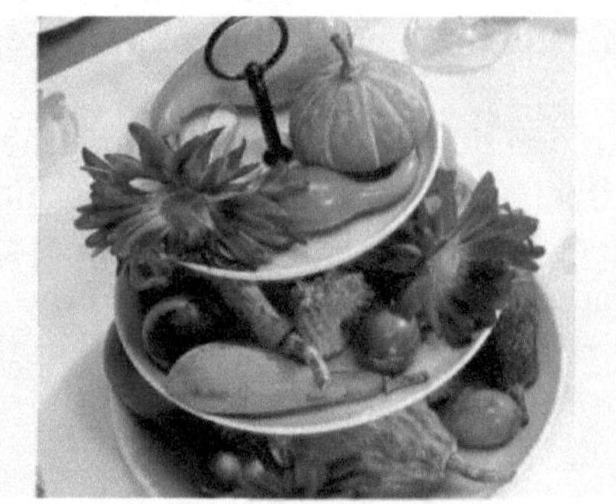

Materials

- 3 layer serving stand
- Gourds and pumpkins in a range of sizes
- Flowers to match
- Clear florist's tubes

Directions

1. Arrange the pumpkins and gourds as it suits you – the larger gourds should be reserved for the lower levels. Check where you

can cover gaps using flowers and place the flowers into the florist's tubes with water so that the last longer. Add in the flower and tubes, trying to keep the tubes out of sight.

Craft 170: Cheery Christmas Tea

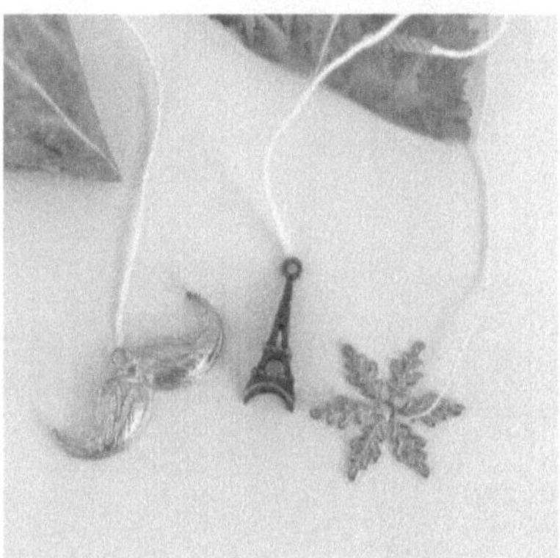

Materials

- Tea bags with tags
- Charms (brightly colored pieces of paper)
- A snowflake punch or other punch
- Christmas themed paper or card
- Scissors
- Super glue
- Jump rings optional

Directions

1. You can either use paper and punches to create your own charms or use the ones that you have already – as long as they go with your theme, the choice is yours. If you are making your own charms, simply choose the paper or card that you like and punch out or cut out the pieces that you want.

2. Once done, punch a small hole in the top of the card and thread your jump ring through (if using them). Cut the tag off your teabag and thread the end of the string through the jump ring/ hole in the new tag/ charm. Tie a neat knot close to the jump ring/ hole and

apply a small dot of super glue to make sure that the knot does not unravel. Trim the edges.

Craft 171: A Timely Perfume Gift

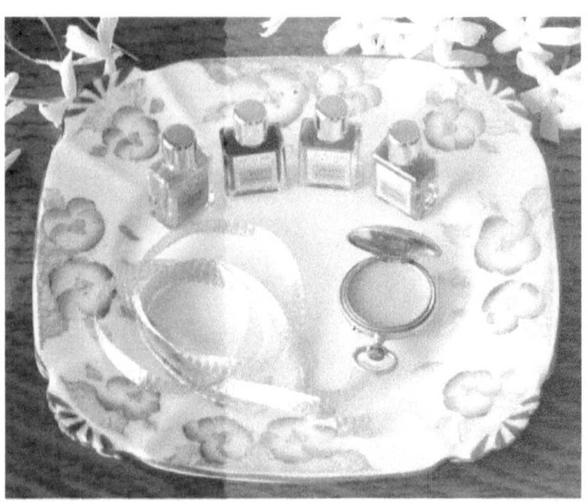

Materials

- 7.5ml jojoba oil
- 5 drops of ylang essential oil
- 5 drops of frankincense essential oil
- 5 drops of ginger essential oil
- 3ml pure beeswax (grated)
- A small pot to melt wax in
- A little cup
- A wooden skewer
- An old pocket watch (insides removed and thoroughly cleaned)

Directions

1. Place the jojoba in the small cup and add in the essential oils. Mix with a wooden skewer until completely combined. Place the beeswax in the microwave on high for 30 seconds so that it melts. If it needs a bit more time, microwave on high at 30 second intervals. As soon as melted, mix into the essential oil/ jojoba oil blend and stir well.

2. Work quickly and put in the microwave for another 10 seconds on high so that it is easier to pour. Pour into the base of the pocket watch and leave to set on a level surface. If necessary, make more to top up the pocket watch.

Craft 172: Christmas Notebook

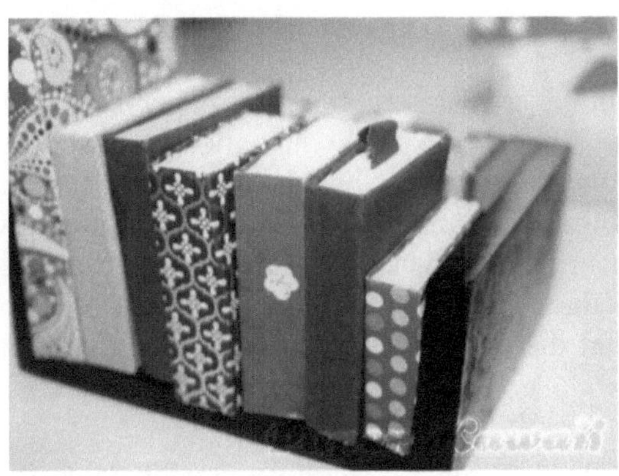

Materials

- 1 Piece pretty scrapbooking paper (6 inches x 6 inches)
- 4 pieces plain white paper (6 inches x 6 inches)
- A paper trimmer (scissors)
- Paper glue
- Lights

Directions

1. For the moment, set the patterned paper to one side. Fold the other sheets of paper in half and cut along this fold line. Fold the sheets in half widthwise once again so that you have a long, thin rectangle of paper. Fold this in half lengthwise. Now fold the top half in half again, back down to the starting point. Flip and repeat on the other side. When you open this out, you will have an accordion fold. Repeat with the other pieces of paper.

2. Take the first folded piece of paper and hold it with the open side facing the table. Grasp the middle fold with your finger, leaving the two outer "pages" free. The page on the left will be tucked into the cover of your book. The page on the right will be tucked into

the next set of pages. Get your second set of pages, also with the open side facing the table and this time, open the left outermost fold a little. Slot this onto the last page of the previous book. Continue in this manner until all the pages have been slotted into each other in this manner, leaving only the outermost pages free. Glue the errant flaps together so that you have a continuous accordion of pages that will not come apart and get ready to make the cover.

3. Take your patterned scrapbooking paper and fold it in half. Cut along the folded line. Fold in half again widthwise to find the center point of the page but do not crease the paper. Using this center point as a guideline, fold the two sides toward the center point, ensuring that there is a gap of around a millimeter between the two edges at the center (to ease the fit of the cover) and also ensure that the pattern that you want to show is on the outside of the fold.

4. Fold the page in the center and put your book along this crease. Make a second crease in a similar fashion so that you create a spine for your book. Place the book into its spine and make a note of where the pages of the book end on your cover. Giving about a millimeter of easement away from this point, crease the paper so that it folds in, like a book jacket would. Repeat on the other side as well. Now take your first "page" and slot it into your book cover. Repeat for the back of the book as well and you are done.

Craft 173: Soap That Looks Good Enough to Eat

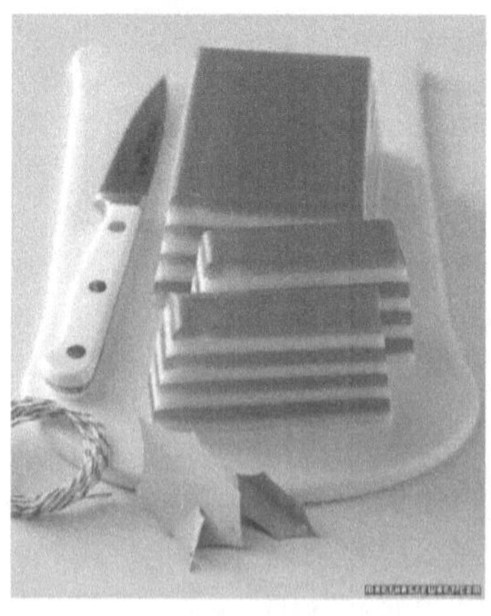

Materials

- Melt-and pour clear glycerin soap
- Peppermint oil or soap scent
- Food colorings in red and green
- Plastic spoon
- A microwave safe jug
- A suitable mold

Directions

1. Split the soap up into batches no larger than about a quarter cup each and cube it. Put the first batch in the microwave and microwave on 80% power for around 30 second bursts until melted. When completely melted, add a drop or two of the peppermint oil and a little red food coloring and stir gently with a spoon until just combined – if you stir too vigorously, you will have more bubbles to contend with. Pour in the first layer and leave to cool for at least 15 minutes. Lightly score the top so that the next layer of soap adheres better.

2. Make the next layer clear or green and follow the process above, this time pouring it over the first layer of soap. Add as many layers as you like and leave to set for a minimum of 4 hours or until completely cool. Your soap is ready for use – as it is glycerin-based, it will sweat if in contact with air so do be sure to wrap in cling wrap as soon as set.

Craft 174: Washied Up Lip Balm

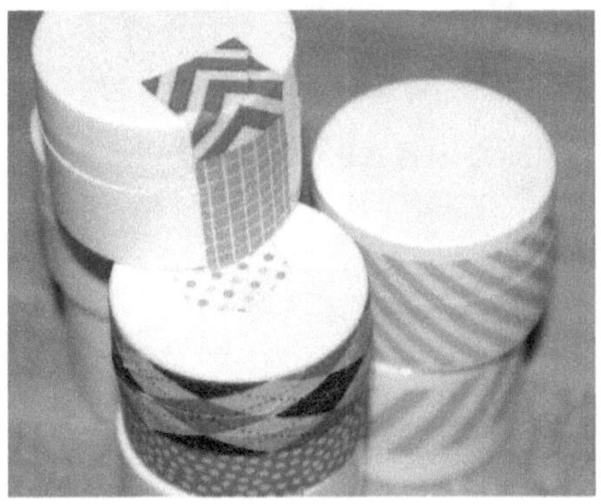

Materials

- 7g cocoa butter
- 7g mango butter
- 7g shea butter
- 30ml beeswax (grated)
- 5ml cosmetic grade scent oil of your choice
- Cosmetic grade colorants and glitter (optional)
- Lip balm pots
- Washi tape

Directions

1. Do be sure to sterilize your equipment and the lip balm pots before you use them. In a microwave safe container, mix the beeswax and oils and butters together and microwave them at about 60% power until they have liquefied. Mix well and add your scents and any colorants that you may be using. If using glitter, add it now. Decant into the lip balm pots, close and set aside to set. If it starts to set before you are ready, simply pop in the microwave for a few seconds. Decorate the container with Christmas-themed Washi tape. Cover the opening with the tape so that people are able to see that the tape has not been opened.

Craft 175: For the Avid Gardener

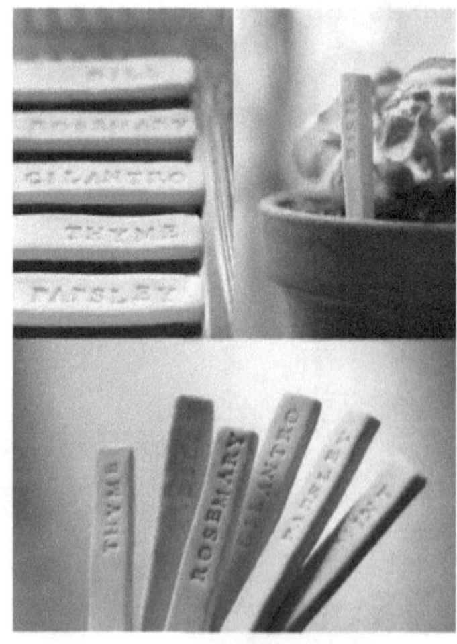

Materials

- Polymer clay that you can bake in the oven
- A baking dish to bake the markers on
- A sturdy rolling pin
- A set of letter stamps (rubber)
- A butter knife
- Your oven

Directions

1. Each marker requires a ball of clay around about 1.25 inches in size so make enough balls to tally with the number of markers that you want to make. Roll each of these balls out so that they are more of a coil and, when it reaches about 5 inches long, flatten out to no more than an eighth of an inch in thickness. Ensure that the markers are all of even shape and size and properly squared off using the flat surface of your knife. End off by trimming the one end of each marker into a point so that you can stake it into the ground.

2. Rub gently to smooth the surface of the cuts as necessary and put the markers on the baking tray and preheat your oven according to the recommendations of the manufacturers. Stamp the required letters on using your stamp set – if you make any errors, you can always start again or try to smooth over them. Bake as required and then set aside to cool completely before using. The markers will be watertight but will not stand up to too much rough handling.

Craft 176: Homely Little Gifts

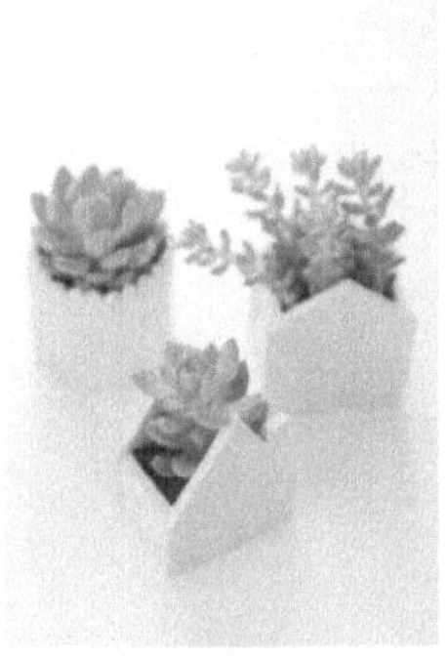

Materials

- A knife
- Clay that you can bake in the oven
- A rolling pin
- Baking paper
- A baking tray
- A ruler (optional)
- A house template found online and cut out (optional)
- A smoothing tool (anything with a sufficiently long handle and smooth surface to smooth out the clay)

Directions

1. Preheat your oven according to the instructions from the manufacturer of the clay. Lay out the baking paper on the tray and roll the clay over it to a thickness of around an eighth of an inch or so. If you are using a template, lay it onto the clay and cut around it with a knife. Alternatively, cut free-hand or use any shape that you want to.

2. You will need to cut one base and four sides for your finished item so do that now. Assemble the pieces one at a time. You can strengthen the pot and also make it less likely to leak by placing a coil of clay over the inside joins. You can then use the smoothing tool to help smooth out the inside of the pot. When the inside has been done, you should flip it over and make sure that the joins on the outside are carefully smoothed over.

3. You can then repeat the procedure with the remaining sides. You will need to support the structure of the clay as you go so that the smoothing process does not cause unsightly bulges. On the bright side, if you do make a mess of it, you can always just squish it up and roll it out again to start from scratch.

4. Place the tray and clay structure into your oven to bake and check on it now and again to ensure that it is doing okay. Once done, set aside and allow to cool completely before filling it with water to ensure that it is indeed watertight.

Craft 177: Button Wreaths

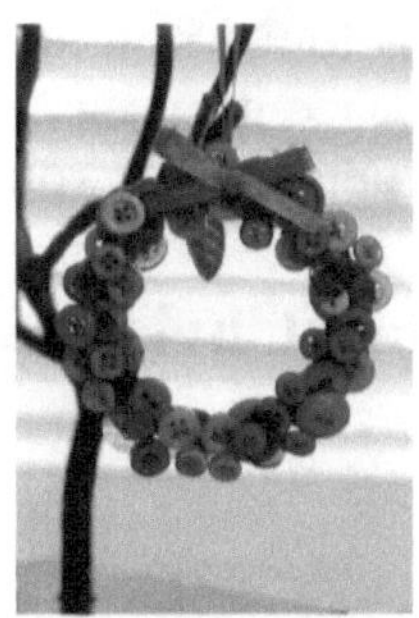

Materials

- Assorted buttons (red, white and green are good)
- 18 gauge craft wire
- Bows to use as a decoration (optional)
- Wire cutters
- A circle template/cup
- Hot glue

Directions

1. Lay out the buttons in groups according to color or pattern – whichever will work for you. Draw your circle template on a piece of paper so that you have a basic idea of what quantities to use. Lay the wire around the outside of the circle and then add another two inches before cutting.

2. Start to thread your buttons on one at a time, each time alternating between a button underneath and a button at the top. This will enable you to lay the wreath flatter later on. You want the buttons to fit snugly together so that the wire will hold its shape. As you are going along, mold the wreath into a circular shape, using your template as a guide.

3. When you are happy with the size and shape of your wreath, close it off and twist the two ends of the wire together securely. If you plan to use the wreath as an ornament, you can use the excess wire to create a loop. Just make sure that the rough edges are tucked away safely. If you like, you can add a drop or two of hot glue at intervals to help your wreath keep its shape – just be careful that it

doesn't drip through the holes in the button as this can mar the effect. Set aside to dry for at least 5 minutes before continuing. If you are applying bows to the front, put a small dab of hot glue on the back of one and place it on the bow as you like. Set aside so that the glue cools completely and you are all done.

Craft 178: Father Christmas Chair Decor

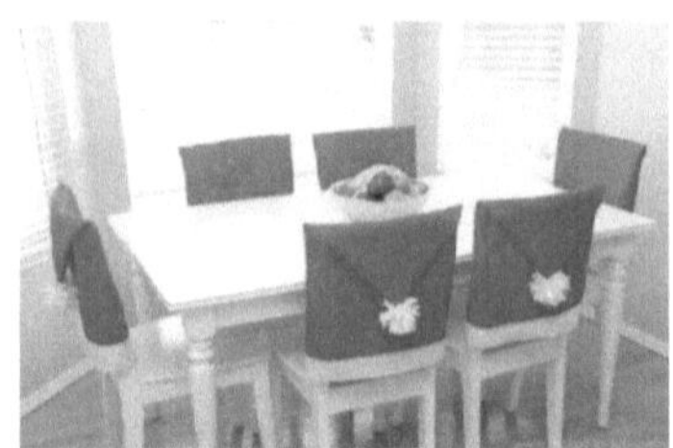

Materials

- Felt (off the bolt and in red and white)
- Matching sewing cottons
- A sewing machine (you can do it by hand if you want to)

Directions

1. You will need to measure how big your chairs are first so that you know how much fabric to buy. You will need to measure how wide the chair is, how thick the back is – the thicker the back of the chair, the more allowances you will need to make. My best tip is to take a bit of scrap fabric or paper and make a mock cover – that will give you the best indication of how much material you will need per chair. It is not a good idea to cover the whole back of the chair – leave about an inch and a half of room between the bottom of the cover and the chair to avoid people sitting on it and pulling it down too far.

2. In addition to the actual chair cover itself, you also need enough fabric for the pointy part of the hat so add another 10 inches of material in length. Cut your red fabric into strips in accordance with the measurements that you took, allowing a seam allowance of at least an inch on all sides. Fold each strip of fabric in half, right sides facing together.

3. Clip off the top two corners of the fabric so that you get the classical triangle shape of the hat. Sew all the edges together, aside from the bottom of the "hat" and clip the seams so that they are less bulky. Hem the bottom edges of your "hat", press and turn the right way around again. Starting at the point that the hat starts to slope upwards, sew a straight line across to the corresponding point in matching red cotton. This will prevent the cover from sliding too far down the back of the chair. Taking your white felt, cut a strip that is around 2.5 inches in width that you can use to trim the hat.

4. Sew the two short ends of the strip together so that you have a band. Attach this band to the bottom hem of your seat cover, ensuring that the side seams match up with one another. Secure by sewing a straight line along the bottom of the strip in white and a second line along the top edge of the strip so that it is held in place securely.

5. Now you need to make your pom-poms. Cut a long strip of felt in white, about a third of an inch in width. Cut these into shorter strips to use to make the pom-pom. Make a pom-pom by securing some strong cotton around the center of the thread. Double knot it so it is secure and fluff out the pom-pom so that it starts to take shape. Secure to the tip of your "hat" using a bit of cotton and some secure running stitches. Double knot to close off and you are done.

Craft 179: Rustic Sign

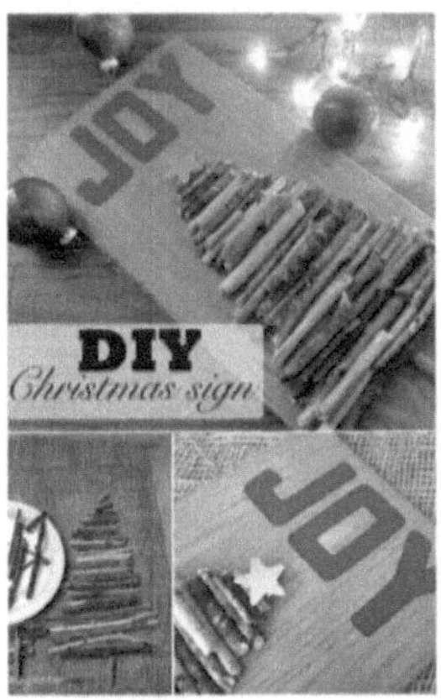

Materials

- Scrap bits of wood (leftover pallet)
- Wood twigs collected from outside
- Sandpaper
- Wood stain if desired
- Acrylic spray paint
- A stencil
- Hot glue

Directions

1. Take the board and cut it to the size that you want. Sand it so that the surface is smooth and stain as required. Set aside to dry. Apply a light coating of spray paint and, before it is properly dry, drag a rag through it to pull of some of the paint. With a pencil, draw a basic center line on the board to use as your guideline for placing the twigs and start gluing them on as necessary. Look and see if there are any holes or gaps that need filling and add in twigs if necessary. Stencil the word of your choice onto the top part of the board and set aside to dry.

2. Finish it off by adding a star for the top of the tree – simply hot glue it into place. If you want a bit more of a decorative effective, consider adding burlap bows or Christmas baubles. Another pretty effect is created by lightly glittering some of the twigs using a clear, fine glitter. Alternatively, some conifer branches in place of bare ones can really change the whole look.

Craft 180: An Alternative to A Door Wreath

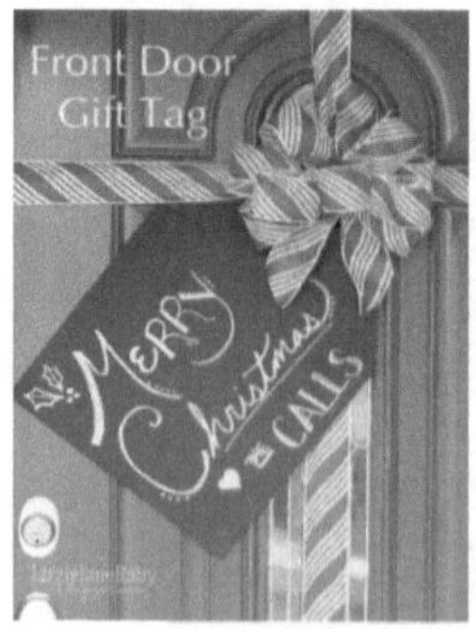

Materials

- Wide ribbon in Christmas colors
- A pipe cleaner
- Black heavy cardstock or plywood painted black
- Something to cut everything with
- Command strips
- A chalk marker or acrylic paint

Directions

1. Start by measuring your door. You will need a length of ribbon that reaches from the top of the door, to the bottom, with a little room left over to allow you to tape it to the top and bottom edge of the door, without actually being visible on the back. You will need a second piece of ribbon that reaches side to side in the same manner. You will also need matching ribbon to create a large bow. Start by taping the ribbon in place and then make your bow. Attach the bow using a pipe cleaner to the center where the two ribbon strips meet.

2. To make the "tag", you can either use heavy black card, 20 inches by 15 inches in size or a similarly sized piece of plywood, painted black. Lop off the top two corners of the "tag" so that it starts to take shape. Using a chalk marker or acrylic paint, write on your message. For a different effect, draw a dotted line all around to give the feeling that the tag has been stitched. You will need to use command strips to adhere it to the door. Tuck the ends under the bow – so it looks as though a gift bag has been tied onto the ribbon.

Craft 181: Cheery Christmas Window

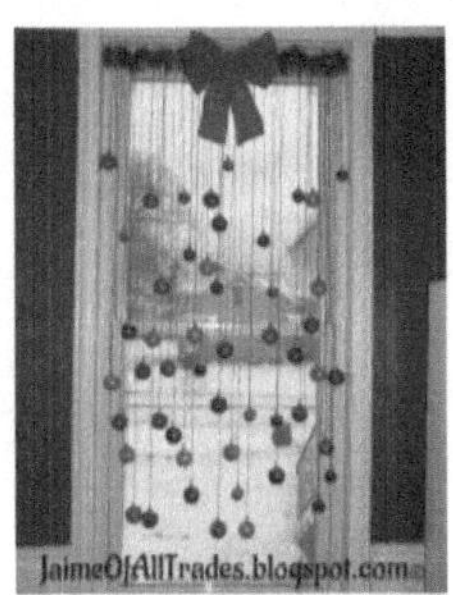

Materials

- Christmas baubles (enough to get the effect that you want)
- A curtain rail or piece of curtain wire that will fit the window
- Good quality tinsel or garlanding
- A big bow
- Scissors
- Fishing wire

Directions

1. Sort the ornaments into groups – start with those that you want to place at the bottom of the window and work your way up, layer by layer. Work on one layer at a time and secure the fishing line first to the end of the ornament and then to the curtain rail. Hang all the other ornaments for that layer in the same manner, adjusting height as necessary. I suggest putting the rail/ wire up in the window first and then adding the ornaments when it is up. Otherwise you will have a huge tangle of wires to contend with later.

2. Carry on until you have completed each layer and are happy with the result. Cover the curtain rail or wire with the tinsel or garlanding and secure in place using the fishing line. Finish off by tying your bow into position.

Craft 182: Rudolph The Mail Box

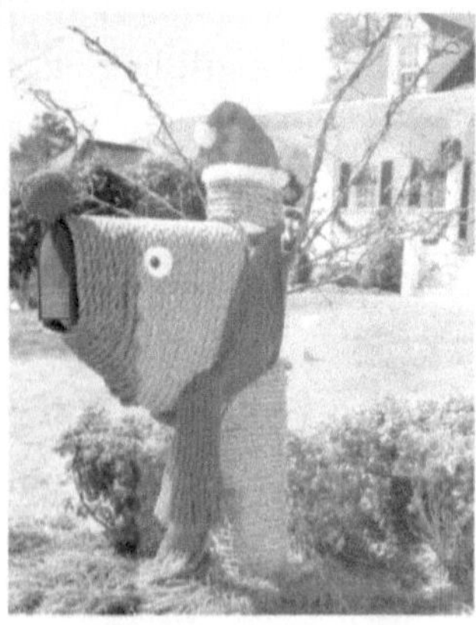

Materials

- Something that will cut through heavy rope and wood
- Outdoor Christmas lights with their own power source
- About 200 feet of rope (at least ½ an inch thick)
- Two tree branches to use as antlers
- Two 3-inch-thick slabs cut from a tree branch
- Acrylic yarn in a bright red color
- A 3-inch ball
- A hot glue gun
- Some stick of hot glue
- A permanent marker
- An old scarf
- White (all-weather paint)
- A paint roller or brush
- 2-inch wood screws (non-corrosive)
- A screwdriver/screw gun
- A drill

Directions

1. This is a two-person job so you will need some help. Start off by positioning the branches so that your mailbox starts looking as though it has antlers. Cut away any extra bits that you do not need and set aside, taking note which was better on which side of the mail box. Drill a hole into the branches, at the spot where they are to be attached to the mail box. Fasten to the post of the mailbox using the wood screws. The Christmas lights can then be wrapped around your antlers.

2. Next up is to cover the post and the mail box with the rope. Starting at the very bottom of the post, tie the rope securely into place. From there, wrap tightly around the post, ensuring that it is properly covered without gaps showing. Continue until the mailbox is covered in a similar manner – remember that you will still need to be able to add or retrieve mail so do not cover the flap completely. Secure the end of the rope with a screw. If necessary, you can hot glue the rungs of the rope to each other to keep them in place when wrapping them. Do be careful just to glue the rope though and not to glue it to the mail box post.

3. Make the eyes using the two pieces of wood. Cut them to about a quarter of an inch in thickness and paint the whites of the eyes on. Set aside to dry and then draw in the pupils with your permanent marker. Hot glue onto the rope on the side of your mail box. Wind the yarn around your ball and glue into place, ensuring that the ball is completely covered. Hot glue the nose into place. Throw the scarf around the neck to finish it off or even considering adding a Father Christmas hat.

Craft 183: Oh, Christmas Tree

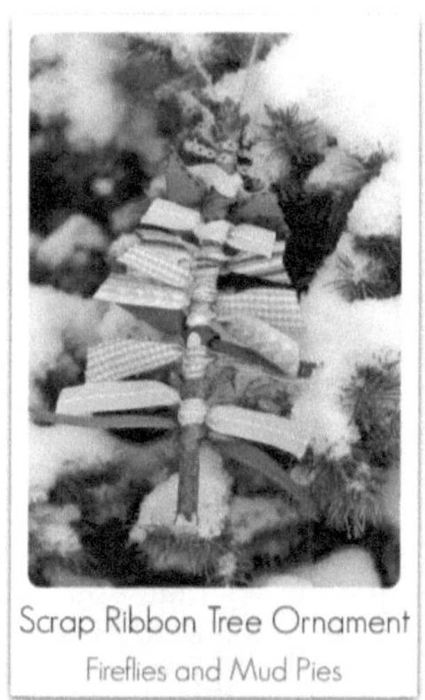

Scrap Ribbon Tree Ornament

Fireflies and Mud Pies

Materials

- Scrap bits of ribbon in Christmas colors
- Some wooden twigs from the garden
- A cord to hand the "tree" on
- A lighter (optional)
- Scissors

Directions

1. Start off by tying on your scraps of ribbon to the tree twig – one twig will form the center of each Christmas tree ornament. At this point, look for a configuration that you like, in place of worrying too much about how long the strips are. If you prefer to do so, you

can also cut the strips to pre-determined lengths and seal them before tying them on, it depends on what kind of time you have. I prefer tying them on and then sealing and trimming them because that gives a far more predictable result.

2. Whichever way you decide to go, heat sealing the ribbon is optional. I prefer doing so because it stops the ribbon from fraying but this must be done with the help of an adult. It is quick and easy, simply pass the end of the ribbon through the flame of the lighter quickly so that it does not catch alight but so that the ends get sealed off. Allow the ribbon to cool for a few seconds before touching to check – synthetic ribbons can retain the heat and cause nasty burns. When you are happy with the ornament, you can bore a small hole in the top to pass the cord through so that you can hang it up. Alternatively, you can also create a loop in the cord and tie to the top of the "tree". Cover this over with your last piece of ribbon.

Craft 184: Do You Believe?

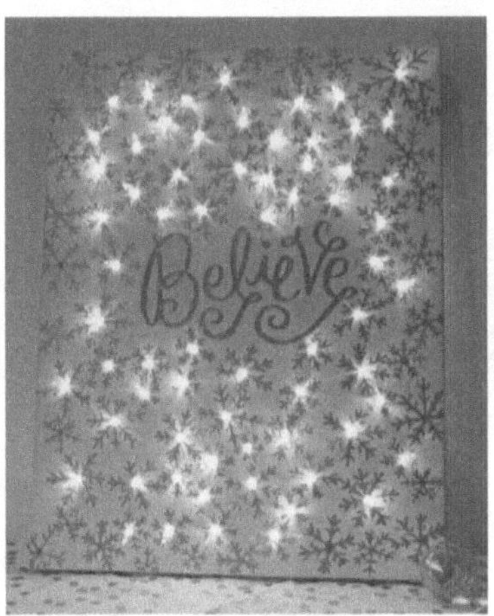

Materials

- A canvas (20 inches by 16 inches)
- A string of at least 100 fairy lights (we used white)
- A sharpie in the color of your choice (we used silver)
- A message for your canvas (a vinyl sticker works like a dream)
- A craft knife

- A holiday-themed stencil (we used snowflakes)
- A pencil
- A hot glue gun (in case necessary)

Directions

1. You could also use a stencil and paint your message onto the canvas but I find that using a vinyl sticker is a whole lot easier. Whichever way you go, decide on the placement of your wording now and make a small mark on the canvas in pencil so that you know where it will go. With the sharpie, stencil in the snowflakes – alternatively, draw them by hand. It is a good idea to mark out where the centers of each flake will be before you fill the whole thing in. Set aside to dry thoroughly.

2. Now it is time to lay your grid of lights. In the center of each flake, punch a hole from the front of the canvas through to the back. It only needs to be big enough for the lights to fit through it. Push a light through each hole. If you mistakenly made a hole too large, secure the light with a little bit of hot glue. Plug it in and check the effect. Adjust as necessary.

Craft 185: Use Your Christmas Ribbon

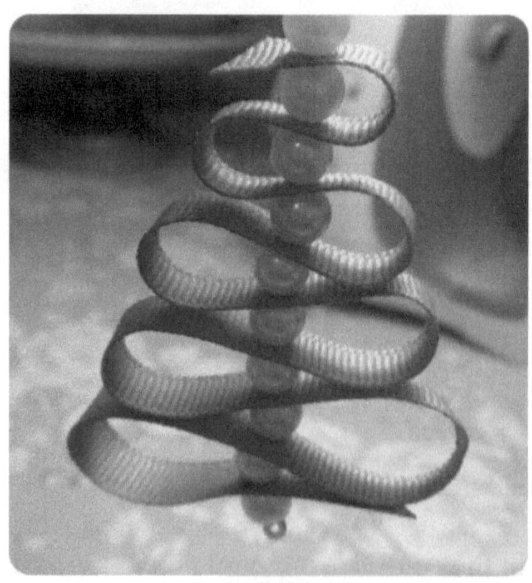

Materials

- Bits of ribbon
- Pearls or other round beads
- Big seed beads
- Scissors
- A lighter or fray check
- A pencil
- Thread in a matching color

Directions

1. You will need around about 19 inches of ribbon per ornament. Seal both ends of the cut ribbon either using the lighter or using fray check and mark out spaces on the ribbon, starting at two and three-quarter inches and decreasing by a quarter of an inch incrementally until you have a piece that is an inch long.

2. Thread a seed bead onto your thread and then add a pearl or round bead. Insert into the first mark on your ribbon. Thread another pearl bead and seed bead on before going back through the second pearl bead and right through the center of all the beads that you put on first. Thread the cotton back up through the first pearl and all the beads following it and then through the second mark on the ribbon.

3. From then on it becomes a lot simpler, simply follow the following sequence – pearl/ round bead, seed bead, and mark on ribbon until done. At the end, leave a one inch length of cord so that you can hang the ornament and thread it back through the last pearl bead added and through the last piece of ribbon. Secure with a neat knot and weave in about an inch of the remaining thread before your cut it.

Craft 186: A Truly Everlasting Tree

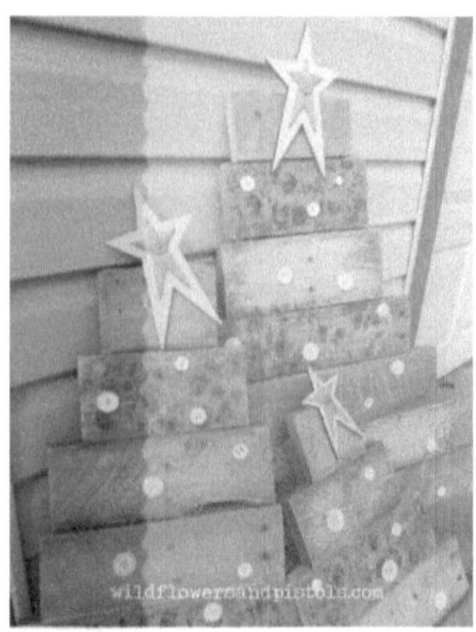

Materials

- An old pallet or scrap pieces of wood
- A saw
- Wood screws
- Serviettes
- Modge Podge
- Chalk paint
- Super glue
- Little buttons (etc. ornaments that you want)

Directions

1. If you have not done so already, you need to tear up your pallet. Keep one of the long boards to act as a tree trunk. You will need to sand the rough edges off but nothing much else to this one. You will then need to cut the "branches" of your tree. This is simply done by cutting strips of the pallet wood to size – until your tree is roughly the shape of a Christmas tree. Screw each board securely in place using wood screws before decorating them.

2. I chose pretty serviettes and split out the top layer printed layer. This layer I applied to the wood with Modge Podge. I finished it off with two layers of Modge Podge to securely coat it – allowing enough time for each layer to dry before applying the next. I alternated serviette decoupage with chalk paint as a means of decorating branches. I diluted the chalk paint quite strongly to get

a thin wash of color and set everything aside to dry. You can attach bows and buttons and whatever else you like with superglue.

Craft 187: Adorable Snowmen

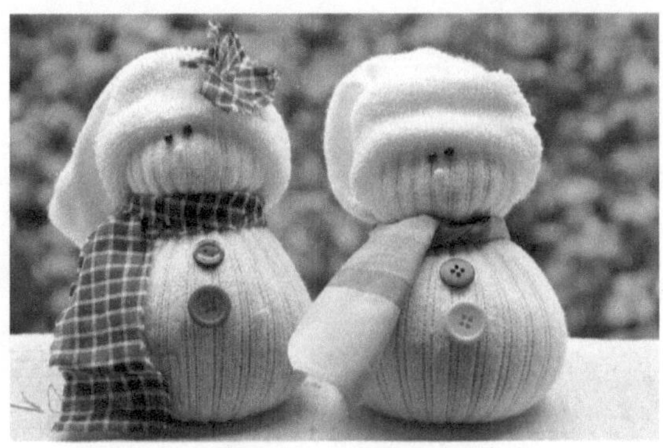

Materials

- A pair of crew length socks (white)
- Scissors
- Yarn
- Buttons
- Embellishments of your choice
- Two map pins, googly eyes or, embroidery cotton
- Felt

Directions

1. Start by cutting off the leg section of the sock and turn it inside out. Grab the top part of the sock and bunch it together. Wrap with yarn to secure and tie off. Pull the sock the right way out before continuing. Now you need to fill the sock – uncooked rice or wheat are good options. Pack the sock nicely so that the base looks good and is not wobbly. Tie off the bottom of the sock and secure well. Tuck it in under the body. Take the top quarter of the filled sock and tie a piece of yarn just below this so that you have a distinct head and body.

2. You can embroider the eyes on or stick in the map pins. Alternatively, hot glue some googly eyes on. You can quickly crochet a small scarf and hat for your snowman or give him

whatever other embellishments you can think of. (Pom-poms make a great set of ear muffs!) You can also use the sock's toe to make a cap for him. Go as mad as you want when it comes to decorating your snowman.

Craft 188: Santa's Own Mason Jar

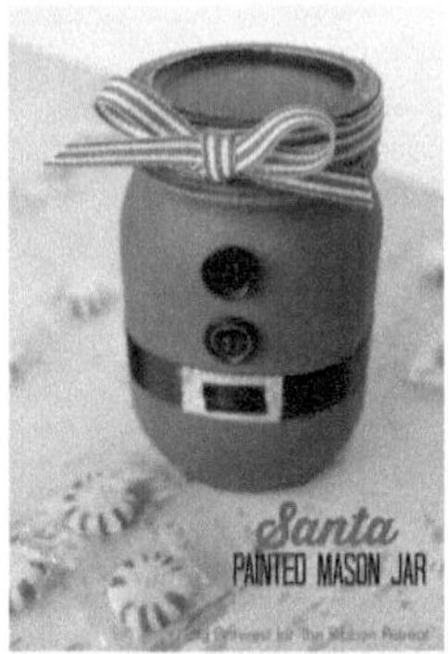

Materials

- Satin ribbon in black
- Metallic ribbon in gold
- Grosgrain ribbon with red and white stripes
- A foam brush
- Acrylic paint in black and red
- A medium sized mason jar and lid
- Buttons in black to match
- A hot glue gun
- Modge Podge

Directions

1. Apply a layer of Modge Podge to the outside of the glass and allow to dry, avoiding the rim of the jar. This makes it easier for the paint to adhere. Again, avoiding the rim of the jar, paint the whole jar red and allow to dry before adding a second coat.

2. You may now paint the rim, ensuring that you do not get any paint on any area that the lid will close on. Paint the lid with a coat of Modge Podge as well. The lid can now be painted black and set aside to dry. Two coats will again be necessary. If you prefer a

glossier finish, finish off with a coat of glossy Modge Podge. Eyeball the middle of the jar and wrap the black ribbon around this point. Glue into place, making sure that the ends overlap exactly so that it is perfect.

3. Using your metallic ribbon, cut a rectangle to form the main part of the buckle, making it a little longer than necessary so that you can glue the edges under so that it is neater and a little raised. Do the same with a piece of black ribbon, ensuring that it is the same width as your "belt". Glue the buttons in place above the buckle so it looks like a button up jacket. Glue a length of the striped ribbon onto the lid, all the way around, ensuring that there is enough at the ends to make a bow. The jar is ready to be filled up with goodies.

Craft 189: Here Comes the Gingerbread Man

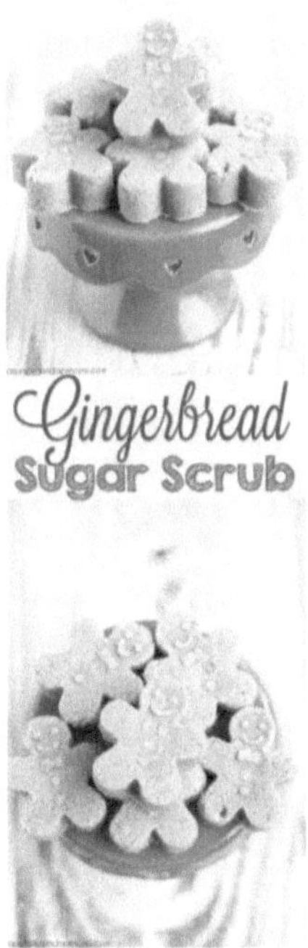

Materials

- 67.5ml sweet almond oil
- 125ml shea butter

- 250ml granulated brown sugar
- 1.75ml vanilla essence
- 1.75ml powdered ginger
- 1.75ml powdered cinnamon
- 1.75ml allspice
- 1.75ml powdered cloves
- A silicon gingerbread man mold

Directions

1. Set up a double boiler on a medium plate and add the Shea butter. Add in the oil and mix until combined. While waiting for the mixture to melt, mix together all the other ingredients aside from the vanilla essence until well combined. Remove the Shea mixture from the heat and add in the vanilla essence. Let it cool for a minute or so and mix in the rest of the ingredients.

2. Spoon the mixture into the mold and pack it tightly into it. You need to work quickly because this will cool off fast. It is best to allow it to set overnight but if you are in a real rush, you can put it in the freezer to set for about half an hour before using.

Craft 190: Spectacular Bauble Tree

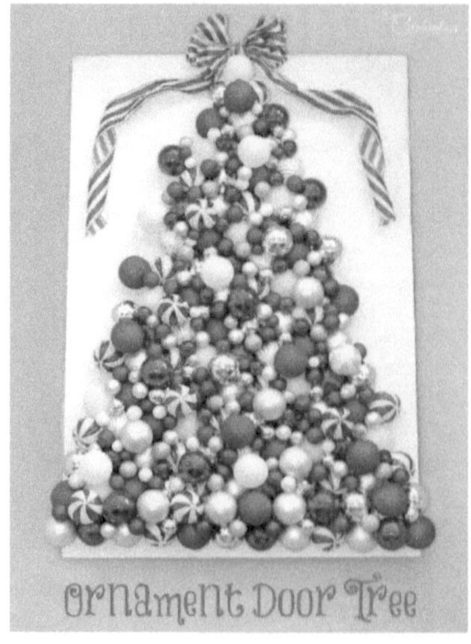

Materials

- A plywood panel
- White acrylic paint
- A pencil
- A ruler
- Christmas ornaments in the color of your theme
- A big bow to match or a Christmas star
- Hot glue

Directions

1. Start off by painting your plywood panel. Allow to dry before applying a second coat of paint. Once this has dried, draw a long, thin triangle in the middle of the board using your pencil. It should resemble a Christmas tree shape. Separate your ornaments in terms of color, shape and size.

2. Starting at the very top of the tree, start to hot glue your baubles over the shape that you drew. You want to keep to the same template but also be sure to cover any pencil lines. Continue until you have covered the whole shape with baubles. (It can be useful to first lay out your baubles before applying the glue to ensure that you are happy with the pattern.)

3. You can now sit back and evaluate the work. To make it even more eye-catching, a second layer of baubles can be really effective. This is not entirely necessary but will make a huge difference. This time, your goal is not to cover the whole of the template but to add in baubles that rest on the small spaces between the first layer of baubles. Carry on until you are happy with the result. Finish it off with a lovely bow or star at the top and you are done.

Craft 191: Deer Head for Christmas

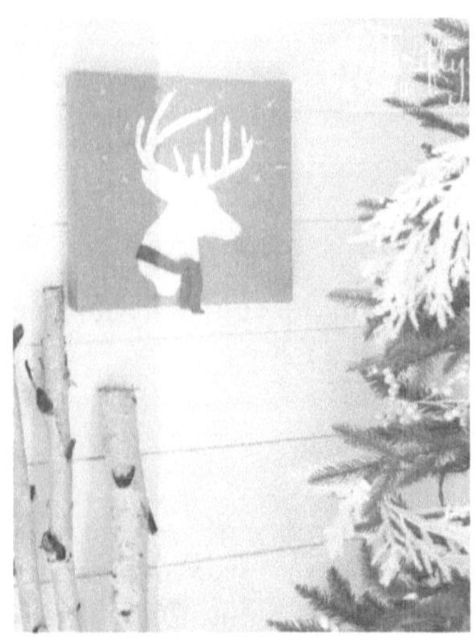

Materials

- A plain deer silhouette stencil
- A plain burlap canvas
- Alternatively get an old picture frame and cover with burlap
- Acrylic paint
- A strand of fairy lights with their own power source
- A craft knife
- A hot glue gun
- Ribbon or felt
- Adhesive tape

Directions

1. Position the stencil as you like on the burlap and paint in the deer's head. Allow to dry undisturbed before removing the stencil. Next you need to mark out where you will put the lights. Cut a hole into these areas just big enough for the fairy lights to poke through and stick the fairy lights in place. Tape the power pack to the inside back of your canvas so that it is both supported and out of the way.

2. Make an incision in the burlap on either side of the deer's neck, about where a scarf would naturally sit. It should be just big enough for the ribbon or felt to fit through. Thread the ribbon or felt through each of the slits made – both ends should end up at the

front of the canvas. Tie into a loose knot and, if using ribbons, heat seal the ends.

Craft 192: Sweet Little Christmas Tray

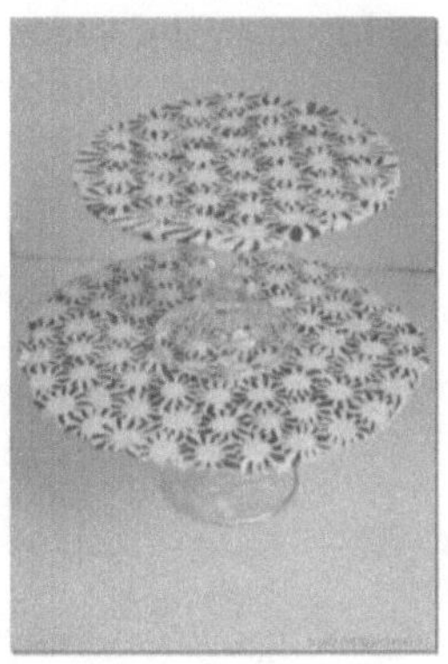

Materials

- 2 packets of round (striped peppermint candies)
- A sheet of non-stick baking paper
- A flat baking tray
- A cake tin with removable base
- Cheap glass or ceramic candle sticks
- A hot glue gun
- Clear varnish (optional)

Directions

1. Set your oven at 325F and allow it to warm up. If your candies have wrappers, unwrap each of them. Set out the baking paper on your baking tray and then remove the bottom from the cake tin. Place the cake tin squarely in the center of the baking sheet. Lay out the candies so that the whole base is covered and set in oven. Carefully remove the cake tin, trying not to disturb the candies.

2. Leave them in for about 9 minutes or so, or until they just melt. You want a solid mass but not a liquid one. Remove the tin from the oven and clean up the edges of the circle as necessary. Set aside to cool completely and then peel the baking paper off. Repeat using a smaller cake tin for the top serving tray. If you like, you

can coat both trays in a clear varnish so that they last a bit longer but this is up to you. (Do keep in mind that the candies may sweat if the temperature in the room is too warm.)

3. Once the varnish is dry, hot glue the center of the bottom base onto the first candlestick. Hot glue the second candlestick to the center of the first base and glue the smaller base to the top of this candlestick.

Craft 193: Vintage Charm

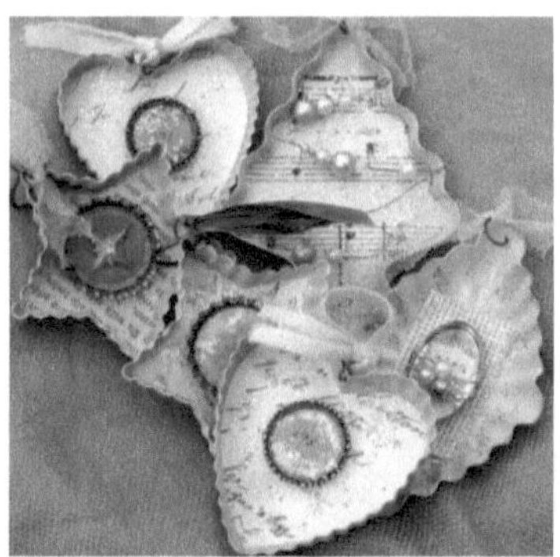

Materials

- Cookie cutters in various shapes and sizes
- Pretty paper in colors of your choosing
- Matching ribbon
- A metal hole punch
- Embellishments as you like
- A hot glue gun
- Acrylic paint to match your paper and ribbon
- Plain washi tape to match your paper
- Jump rings
- Glitter
- A craft knife or scissors

Directions

1. Set out the cookie cutters on your paper, framing whatever sections you like. Trace around the outside and either cut out with scissors or your craft knife. Set the cutouts aside for the moment. Paint the

cookie cutters in the color of your choice and set aside to dry. Apply a second coat to the inside as necessary and allow to dry. Punch a hole in the top of the cookie cutter.

2. Choose your embellishments and figure out how they will be adhered to the paper or cookie cutter. If, for example, you plan to use a beaded cord, you are going to need to adhere it to the cookie cutter rather than the paper. Lay any string or lace elements across the back of the cookie cutters before placing the paper cutouts in place. Adhere everything securely using washi tape and paint a second coat of paint on the sides of the stencil to make the tape less obvious. Add another coat in need. Glue whatever other embellishments you might like to the paper cutouts themselves using hot glue. Sprinkle with a coat of glitter for some extra sparkle. Thread the jump rings through the holes and tie ribbons through these and hang as you like.

Craft 194: Sweet Lights

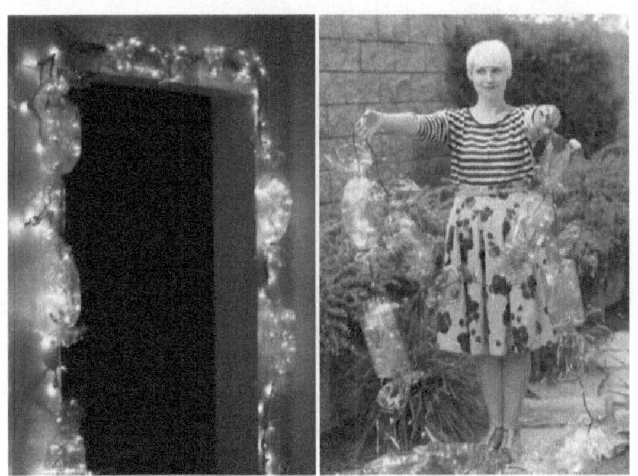

Materials

- Clear corsage boxes (as many as you like)
- A strand of fairy lights
- Thin craft wire or fishing line to secure
- Wire cutters (if using wire)
- Scissors
- Cellophane in bright colors
- Adhesive tape

Directions

1. Cut squares of cellophane that measure roughly 18 inches by 18 inches. Wrap some of the lights in this cellophane so that both ends of the cord are left free. Secure the cellophane loosely and then bundle this up into a corsage box. Tape it shut.

2. Cut your next piece of cellophane in the same color but about double the size so that it can be wrapped around the box as a candy wrapper. When you are happy with the effect, tape the edges together, just where the cellophane and box edges meet. Skip about three lights and then make your next candy in the same manner. Carry on until your strand is as long as you want.

Craft 195: Happy Happy Snowmen

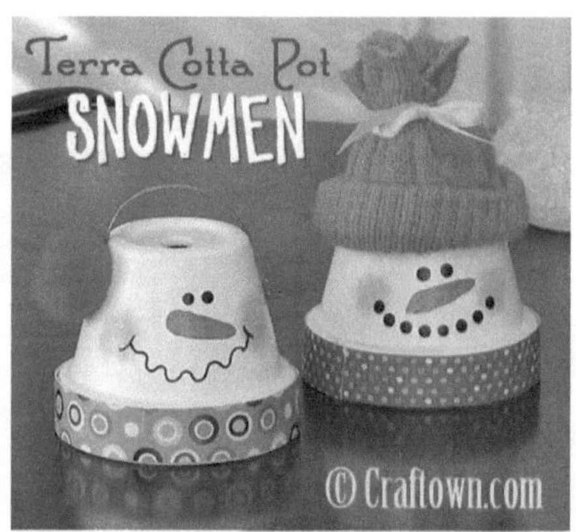

Materials

- Plain garden pots in terra cotta
- Various acrylic paint colors
- Pretty scrapbook paper
- White craft glue
- Scissors
- A permanent marker in black
- A set of pompons and matching ribbon and craft wire or
- An old sock or glove
- Hot glue

Directions

1. Turn the pots upside down and coat with a layer of white paint – leaving the rim of the pot fairly paint-free. Allow to dry and add a second coat as necessary. Paint on eyes and a nose for your snowman, using the marker for outlines as necessary. Take your scrapbooking paper and trim to fit the rim of the pot. Glue in place with the white craft glue.

2. If you are going to give your snowman ear muffs, cut a length of craft wire that will reach from ear to ear, allowing for a slightly rounded effect so that they look more like ear muffs. Wrap in ribbon and hot glue to the pot using a dollop of glue. While the glue is still hot, press on the pompons to further secure the wire.

3. If you are going to make the hat, cut the foot or fingers off your sock or gloves, turn inside out and tie up the cut end with a piece of string. Turn right way round and put the hat on the snowman. Alternatively, you can put directly onto the snowman after having cut the foot/ fingers off and secure this with a ribbon to decorate.

Craft 196: Reindeer Ornament

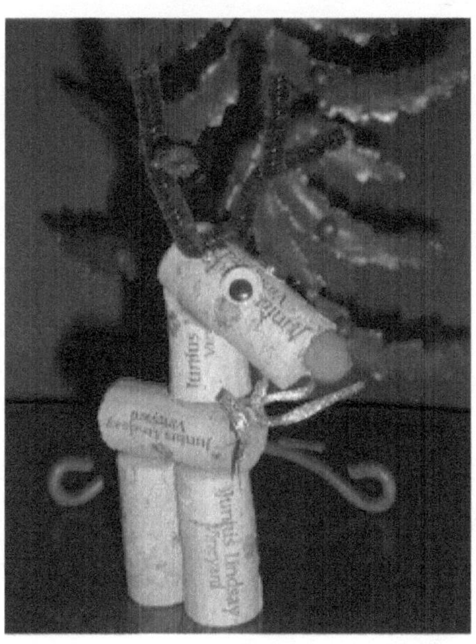

Materials

- 5 wine corks
- A pompon for the nose
- A set of googly eyes
- A brown pipe cleaner
- A pretty little bow
- A hot glue gun
- A sharp knife

Directions

1. Lay out all the corks. Set one aside for the neck. This one you will cut at an angle so that the neck is shapelier. Glue a cork to the angle side to form the head. Glue a second cork to the flat side to form the body.

2. Glue the last two corks in place underneath the body to form legs. On the head, hot glue the googly eyes and pompon nose into place. Add the bow as well. The antler part is the most complicated bit. Cut the pipe cleaner in half and twist each half into an antler shape. Hot glue onto the reindeer and you are done.

Last Chance to Get YOUR Bonus!

FOR A LIMITED TIME ONLY – Get my best-selling book "DIY Crafts: The 100 Most Popular Crafts & Projects That Make Your Life Easier" absolutely FREE!

Readers who have downloaded the bonus book as well have seen the greatest changes in their crafting abilities and have expanded their repertoire of crafts – so it is *highly recommended* to get this bonus book today!

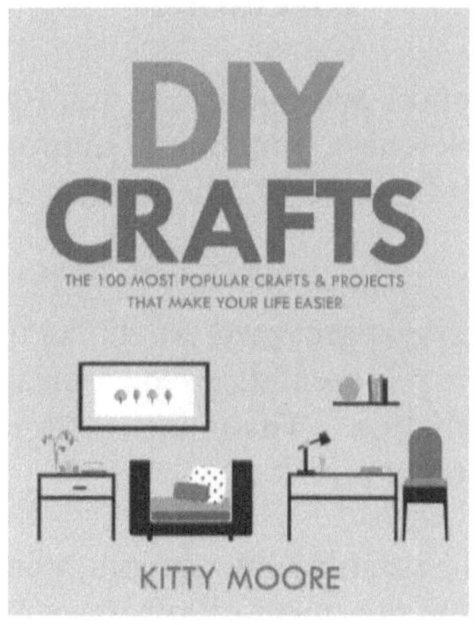

Get your free copy at:

ArtsCraftsAndMore.com/Bonus

Final Words

Thank you for downloading this book!

I really hope that you have been inspired to create your own projects and that you will have a lot of fun crafting.

I do hope that you and your family have found lots of ways to fill lazy afternoons or rainy days in a more fun way.

If you have enjoyed this book and would like to share your positive thoughts, could you please take 30 seconds of your time to go back and give me a review on my Amazon book page!

I really appreciate these reviews because I like to know what people have thought about the book.

Again, thank you and have fun crafting!

Disclaimer

No Warranties: The authors and publishers don't guarantee or warrant the quality, accuracy, completeness, timeliness, appropriateness or suitability of the information in this book, or of any product or services referenced by this site.

The information in this site is provided on an "as is" basis and the authors and publishers make no representations or warranties of any kind with respect to this information. This site may contain inaccuracies, typographical errors, or other errors.

Liability Disclaimer: The publishers, authors, and other parties involved in the creation, production, provision of information, or delivery of this site specifically disclaim any responsibility, and shall not be held liable for any damages, claims, injuries, losses, liabilities, costs, or obligations including any direct, indirect, special, incidental, or consequences damages (collectively known as "Damages") whatsoever and howsoever caused, arising out of, or in connection with the use or misuse of the site and the information contained within it, whether such Damages arise in contract, tort, negligence, equity, statute law, or by way of other legal theory.